CHARCUTERIE BY OCCASION

This book may be ordered by mail from the publisher. Please include $5.99 for postage and handling.

Please support your local bookseller first!

Books published by Cider Mill Press Book Publishers are available at special discounts for bulk purchases in the United States by corporations, institutions, and other organizations. For more information, please contact the publisher.

Cider Mill Press Book Publishers
"Where good books are ready for press"
501 Nelson Place
Nashville, Tennessee 37214

cidermillpress.com

Typography: Aktiv Grotesk, Aktiv Grotesk Condensed, Fino Sans
Image Credits: All images courtesy of Alejandra Diaz-Imlah.

Printed in Malaysia
24 25 26 27 28 OFF 5 4 3 2 1
First Edition

CHARCUTERIE BY OCCASION

50 VERSATILE SEASONAL SPREADS

ALEJANDRA DIAZ-IMLAH
JAMISON DIAZ-IMLAH

CIDER MILL PRESS

BOOK
PUBLISHERS

CONTENTS

INTRODUCTION 6

SPRING 13

SUMMER 65

FALL 117

WINTER 195

APPENDIX 240

INDEX 249

INTRODUCTION

Welcome to the world of culinary art, where every occasion is an opportunity to create a delicious charcuterie spread. In this book, we will take you on a flavorful journey through a carefully curated collection of recipes, each designed to transform your gatherings into experiences.

This cookbook is your ultimate guide to creating stunning and delicious boards that will leave a lasting impression on your guests. Whether you are a seasoned entertainer looking to take your parties to the next level or a beginner eager to learn the art of charcuterie, the following pages have something special in store for you. From intimate gatherings to grand celebrations, these recipes will help you strike the right note each and every time.

As you'll start to see, a charcuterie board is more than just a matter of arranging meats and cheeses. It's a way of telling a story through food, combining flavors, textures, and colors to set the proper tone and reflect the true spirit of an occasion.

When you start to work through these recipes and curate the boards at home, you'll suddenly find yourself familiar with the art of balancing flavors, selecting the perfect accompaniments, and displaying them in a manner that sparks conversation and ignites appetites. Soon, you'll see that charcuterie is more than just food; it's about people sharing in one another's joy, about connection, and about elevating the everyday until it becomes memorable.

CREATING THE PERFECT BOARD

Selecting the ingredients for a charcuterie board involves a thoughtful balance of flavors, textures, and imagination. Here's a step-by-step guide to help you curate a delightful assortment.

Consider the Occasion: Think about the setting for your board. Is it for a casual gathering, an elegant soirée, or a themed event? The occasion will have considerable influence on what's suitable.

Choose a Variety of Meats: Aim for a diverse selection of cured meats to cater to different palates. Include a mix of styles, flavors, and origins. Common options include:

- **Prosciutto:** Delicate, buttery, and slightly salty
- **Salami:** Spicy, bold, and often featuring a rich garlic flavor
- **Chorizo:** Smoky and slightly spicy
- **Capicola:** Dry-cured pork shoulder that is marbled and flavorful
- **Sausages:** A variety of options, from smoky and spicy to herb-infused

Incorporate Different Cheeses: Offer a range of cheeses with varying textures and tastes. Consider including one cheese from each of the following groups for each and every board:

- **Soft Cheese:** Brie, Camembert, Goat Cheese, Burrata
- **Semi-Hard Cheese:** Cheddar, Gouda, Manchego
- **Hard Cheese:** Parmesan, Pecorino, Aged Gruyère
- **Blue Cheese:** Roquefort, Gorgonzola, Stilton

Balance Flavors and Textures: Ensure a harmonious mix of flavors by pairing salty meats with milder cheeses. Include a mix of textures, from creamy and soft to firm and crumbly.

Consider Regional Specialties: Consider showcasing charcuterie from different regions for an authentic experience. Offerings from Italian, Spanish, French, and other global cuisines can add an exciting twist to a board.

Accompaniments are Key: Select accompaniments that complement and enhance the charcuterie and cheese you have selected. These can include:

- **Breads and Crackers:** Slices of baguette, artisanal crackers, and crostini
- **Fruits:** Fresh grapes, figs, apple slices, and dried fruits
- **Nuts:** Marcona almonds, walnuts, pecans, and hazelnuts
- **Spreads:** Mustards, jams, honey, and chutneys
- **Olives:** A mix of marinated olives will supply tangy and salty notes
- **Pickles:** Cornichons, pickled onions, or any pickled vegetables

Experiment and Personalize: Feel free to experiment with unique or seasonal items. Personalize the board with your favorite selections (though don't go overboard—make sure there's plenty of options that your guests will enjoy).

Quantities and Portions: Plan on using around 2 to 3 oz. of charcuterie per person for a board. Adjust quantities based on the number of guests, who is coming over, and what other food you are serving.

Remember, creating a charcuterie board is an art form that reflects your creativity and taste. Feel free to adapt and evolve your selections based on the feedback and reactions of your guests.

PAIRING INGREDIENTS WITH OCCASIONS & THEMES

We're all about curating a charcuterie board to fit an occasion or theme—it's a good way to get your imagination going, and it will certainly get your guests talking. We have 50 occasions included in this book, but here's a quick guide to help you determine what ingredients may fit a specific gathering.

For a casual, outdoor gathering: Opt for a mix of flavors that evokes a relaxed atmosphere, for

example, salami with cheddar cheese and familiar, comforting accompaniments such as a baguette and/or roasted nuts.

For a sophisticated evening: Choose premium options and pair them with complementary flavors, for example, prosciutto with aged Manchego and elevated accompaniments such as artisanal crackers and dried fruit.

For a romantic night: Craft an intimate board featuring delicate flavors and eye-catching elements, for example, capicola with brie and accompaniments such as dark chocolate, fresh fruit, and edible flowers.

For a fall gathering: Embrace the need for warmth and comfort with rich, earthy, and comforting elements such as smoked sausage with goat cheese and accompaniments such as apple chips, pumpkin seeds, and walnuts.

For a holiday extravaganza: Celebrate the season with festive and indulgent choices, for example, pork pâté with cranberry-crusted goat cheese and decadent accompaniments such as candied pecans and cookies.

STYLING A CHARCUTERIE BOARD

Selecting the right board to present charcuterie upon is essential to creating an inviting and appealing spread. Here's a guide to help you pick the perfect board:

Size and Shape: Choose a board that matches the size of your gathering and the amount of charcuterie you plan to serve. Rectangular, round, and oval boards are common choices. Consider the available space and the number of guests to ensure everyone gets a taste.

Material: Charcuterie boards come in a variety of materials, each with its own aesthetic and functional qualities:

- **Wooden Boards:** Rustic and versatile, wooden boards add warmth. Opt for hardwoods like acacia, maple, or walnut.

- **Slate or Stone:** These provide a contemporary, elegant backdrop for your spread. They're also great for writing on, allowing you to identify the items.

- **Marble:** Luxurious and cool, marble is excellent for keeping cheeses and meats at the proper temperature.

- **Bamboo:** Sustainable and lightweight, bamboo boards offer a unique look.

Texture and Finish: Consider the texture and finish of the board. Some are smooth and polished, while others retain a more natural-feeling surface. The finish should complement the overall theme of your presentation.

Complementary Aesthetics: Your board should harmonize with the overall theme and style of your event. Consider the colors, patterns, and materials of your table settings, serving utensils, and overall décor.

Easy to Clean: Opt for a board that is easy to clean and maintain. Some materials might require special care, while others can simply be wiped off and put away.

Space for Arrangement: Make sure your chosen board has ample space for your selections without being overcrowded. You want each element to stand out and be easily accessible.

Personal Preference: Trust your instincts and personal style when selecting a board. It's an opportunity to express your creativity and showcase your taste.

Consider the Charcuterie: Keep in mind the size and shape of the charcuterie items you plan to serve. A board that can accommodate a variety of shapes and sizes will help you create the most attractive arrangement.

In summary, always remember that the board is a functional element and a canvas for your vision. As it is capable of enhancing the overall presentation and setting the tone, it is just as crucial as the items that go upon it.

ASSEMBLING A CHARCUTERIE BOARD

When preparing a charcuterie board, gathering all your ingredients nearby is essential. Choose a variety of high-quality meats, cheeses, crackers, breads, nuts, fruits, and vegetables to provide a range of flavors and textures. Once you have your ingredients, select a focal point for your board. You may want to highlight a particular cheese or meat or create a color scheme with your ingredients.

To build the board, divide it into sections and consider layering your ingredients. Feel free to mix and match different components, but always aim to create a balanced combination of flavors. When arranging your elements, try scattering them around the board rather than grouping them for a more visually appealing display. You can also get creative with small bowls, ramekins, and garnishes, adding various heights, color, and decorative elements to your board.

Follow these tips, and you're certain to create a stunning charcuterie board that will impress your guests.

SPRING

Too often, the relief that winter has passed eclipses the brilliance that starts to unfurl right under our noses. As the world moves into its period of regeneration, we recommend taking some time to sit back and appreciate the miracle that arrives at the end of each and every winter: spring. What better way to ensure that you take this time than putting together one of these light, fresh-tasting boards and inviting your loved ones over. Trust us—sitting around with your loved ones and enjoying delicious food as you gaze out at the world coming back to life, you can't help but become a little more optimistic about the state of things.

RETURN OF SPRING BOARD

The real key to nailing this board is to keep the flavors bright and fresh so it can really capture the joy and excitement of the world returning to life after the far-too-long dormant period.

YIELD: 6 to 8 Servings

Crackers or bread, as desired

4 oz. brie cheese

4 oz. fresh strawberries, quartered

6 oz. prosciutto or country ham

6 oz. capicola

4 oz. Pickled Asparagus (see page 17)

4 oz. Rhubarb Chutney (see page 16)

4 oz. burrata, halved

3 oz. dried apricots

Marigold petals, for garnish

Fresh herbs (basil, parsley, oregano), for garnish

Candied blood oranges, for garnish

Chive blossoms, for garnish

1 Section the board into three parts, placing crackers in the middle, the brie and some strawberries on the right side, and the prosciutto, capicola, and Pickled Asparagus on the left.

2 Place the Rhubarb Chutney in a small ramekin and place it beside the brie.

3 Place the burrata at the top of the board, next to the crackers.

4 Fill in any gaps with dried apricots and the remaining strawberries. Top the board with the garnishes and enjoy.

RHUBARB CHUTNEY

Yield: 1¼ Cups

Active Time: 25 Minutes

Total Time: 1 Hour and 30 Minutes

½ cup sugar

½ cup water

2 cups diced rhubarb

½ teaspoon chopped fresh ginger

¼ teaspoon turmeric

Zest and juice of 2 lemons

½ teaspoon cinnamon

¼ cup golden raisins

½ teaspoon kosher salt

3 whole cloves

¼ teaspoon cardamom

1 Place the sugar and water in a small saucepan and bring to a boil, stirring to dissolve the sugar.

2 Add the remaining ingredients and stir to combine. Reduce the heat to low and cook until the rhubarb has become soft and most of the liquid has evaporated, about 10 minutes, stirring occasionally.

3 Transfer the mixture to a blender and let it cool briefly.

4 Pulse until the chutney has the desired texture and let it cool completely before serving.

PICKLED ASPARAGUS

Yield: 1 Quart
Active Time: 25 Minutes
Total Time: 24 Hours

1½ cups water

¾ cup rice vinegar

½ cup plus 1 tablespoon sugar

3 tablespoons kosher salt

1 lb. asparagus, trimmed

2 oz. fresh basil

Zest of 1 lemon

1. Place the water, vinegar, sugar, and salt in a small saucepan and bring it to a simmer over medium heat, stirring to dissolve the sugar and salt.

2. Cut the asparagus so that it fits into the mason jar you are using. Place it in the mason jar and add the basil and lemon zest.

3. Pour the brine into the jar and gently stir.

4. Put a lid on the mason jar, but do not fully tighten it. Chill the pickled asparagus in the refrigerator overnight before serving.

DATE NIGHT BOARD

This board is designed for a romantic evening with your special someone. Charcuterie and cheese remove any possibility of hanger to help you focus on one another, and to escalate the passion, there's a Champagne-centered cocktail and oysters.

Yield: 2 Servings

2 oz. pepperoni

2 oz. prosciutto

2 oz. brie cheese

2 oz. chocolate-covered almonds

2 oz. strawberries

2 oz. dried cranberries

Marigolds or other flowers, for garnish

6 to 8 fresh oysters, shucked, for serving

¼ cup Cucumber Mignonette Sauce (see page 21), for serving

2 Raspberry & Rose Sgroppini (see page 22), for serving

1   Select a small board. Fold the pepperoni in half and place it on one side of the board. Arrange the prosciutto beside the pepperoni.

2   Place the brie, chocolate-covered almonds, strawberries, and dried cranberries on the other side of the prosciutto.

3   Garnish the board with marigolds and serve with the oysters, Cucumber Mignonette Sauce, and Raspberry & Rose Sgroppini.

CUCUMBER MIGNONETTE SAUCE

Yield: 4 Servings
Active Time: 5 Minutes
Total Time: 5 Minutes

2 tablespoons minced shallots

⅓ cup peeled and minced cucumber

½ teaspoon kosher salt

¼ teaspoon black pepper

Zest of 1 lemon

⅛ teaspoon Worcestershire sauce

⅛ teaspoon Tabasco

¼ cup Champagne vinegar

2 teaspoons honey

1 Place the shallots and cucumber in a bowl, add the salt, pepper, lemon zest, Worcestershire sauce, and Tabasco, and stir to combine.

2 Add the vinegar and stir to combine. Add the honey and stir to combine. Taste, adjust the seasoning as necessary, and serve.

RASPBERRY & ROSE SGROPPINO

Yield: 1 Drink
Active Time: 5 Minutes
Total Time: 5 Minutes

2 oz. raspberry sorbet

¾ oz. vodka

½ oz. ginger liqueur

¼ oz. freshly squeezed lemon juice

3 oz. Prosecco

½ teaspoon rosewater

1   Place the sorbet in a Champagne flute.

2   Add the vodka, ginger liqueur, and lemon juice and swirl slightly to mix.

3   Pour 1 to 2 oz. of Prosecco into the flute so that the sorbet dissolves.

4   Once the bubbling slows down, add the rest of the Prosecco and the rosewater and enjoy.

MOTHER'S DAY BOARD

A thoughtful and beautiful tribute to mothers everywhere. The key here is keeping it simple and letting the eye-catching Salami Roses steal the show. Of course, that shouldn't stop you from swapping out any of the suggestions below for whatever Mom prefers.

Yield: 6 to 8 Servings

5 oz. Boursin cheese

4 Salami Roses (see page 26)

4 oz. rosemary & sea salt crackers

4 oz. Manchego cheese, sliced

2 oz. dried cherries

Marigolds, for garnish

Oregano blossoms, for garnish

Dill blossoms, for garnish

Thai Basil blossoms, for garnish

Fresh sage, for garnish

1   Place the Boursin in the middle of the board and arrange the Salami Roses around it.

2   Place the crackers and Manchego around the edges of the board.

3   Fill in any gaps with dried cherries, garnish with the flowers and sage, and enjoy.

SALAMI ROSES

Yield: 4 Roses
Active Time: 10 Minutes
Total Time: 10 Minutes

40 slices of Genoa salami

1 Grab a wineglass or a Champagne flute and place it on your countertop. Take a slice of salami and place half of it inside the glass. The other half should hang over the outside of the rim.

2 Place another slice of salami over the first slice so that it overlaps a quarter or half of the first one. Repeat the process with the rest of the salami until there is no visible hole in the middle.

3 Place your palm on top of the glass and carefully flip it over so that the rose gently falls out and use as desired.

BURGER NIGHT BOARD

That first truly warm day in spring is a great time to fire up the grill and indulge in some burger bliss. This board takes its cue from that indelible feeling when smoke and warmth fill the air, and there isn't a single thing wrong in the world.

Yield: 4 to 6 Servings

4 (6 to 8 oz.) grilled beef patties

4 slices of aged gouda cheese

2 oz. red onion, sliced thin

1 tomato, sliced

¼ cup OTL Burger Sauce (see page 30)

3 oz. Bread & Butter Pickles (see page 71)

½ cup Bacon Jam (see page 31)

4 sesame seed buns, for serving

1 Place the patties in the top right corner of the board. Place the cheese and onion beside them.

2 Place a slice of tomato in the center of the board and arrange the rest in a line that reaches the end of the board.

3 Place the burger sauce in a small ramekin and the pickles in another one. Place them on opposite sides of the board.

4 Place the jam in a small bowl, place it in the bottom left corner of the board, serve with sesame seed buns, and enjoy.

OTL BURGER SAUCE

Yield: 1½ Cups
Active Time: 5 Minutes
Total Time: 5 Minutes

1 cup mayonnaise

¼ cup hot sauce

2 tablespoons ketchup

1 teaspoon prepared horseradish

1 teaspoon Worcestershire sauce

Zest of 1 lemon

½ teaspoon kosher salt

1 tablespoon chopped pickles

2 dashes of fresh black pepper

1 tablespoon chopped fresh chives

1   Place all of the ingredients in a bowl and whisk to combine.

2   Taste, adjust the seasoning as necessary, and use as desired.

Yield: ½ Cup
Active Time: 25 Minutes
Total Time: 1 Hour

4 oz. bacon, diced

2 oz. yellow onion, diced

1 oz. brown sugar

1 tablespoon maple syrup

1 tablespoon molasses

2 tablespoons apple cider vinegar

2 dashes of Worcestershire sauce

2 dashes of Tabasco

BACON JAM

1   Place the bacon in a medium saucepan and cook it over medium heat until it is starting to brown, about 5 minutes, stirring occasionally.

2   Pour out all but about 1 tablespoon of the bacon fat, add the onion, and reduce the heat to low. Cook, stirring occasionally, until the onion is translucent, about 4 minutes.

3   Add the brown sugar, maple syrup, and molasses and cook, stirring continually, until the sugar has melted and the mixture is syrupy.

4   Raise the heat to medium. Once the syrup begins to bubble, slowly stream in the vinegar, Worcestershire sauce, and Tabasco.

5   Reduce the heat to low and simmer the jam until it starts to thicken, 10 to 15 minutes, stirring occasionally.

6   Remove the jam from heat, taste it, and season it as necessary. Let the jam cool to room temperature before serving.

EAT & MINGLE CHARCUTERIE CUPS

Yes, this is not a "board," but it's a chance for you to see just how much room there is to play in the charcuterie space, transforming the beloved board experience into a convenient, handheld delight, allowing guests to bounce around the room while enjoying bites of artisanal cheeses thoughtfully paired with cured meats and bread. Keep in mind that what's listed below is only for 1 cup; multiply by however many people you're expecting.

Yield: 1 Cup

1 to 2 slices of bread

2 slices of Manchego cheese

8 slices of salami

3 cubes of feta cheese

4 to 6 olives

2 to 3 crackers

Fresh rosemary, for garnish

Marigolds, for garnish

1   Place the largest items, such as the bread and Manchego, in a cup.

2   Skewer the salami, feta, and olives on toothpicks. Add them to the cup.

3   Add the crackers and garnishes to the cup and enjoy.

BLUE NIGHTS BOARD

After the darkness of winter, the return of light well into the evening is always a welcome sight, a reminder of the difficulty that has passed, and the exuberance to come. Spend a night watching the sun go down and soaking up those hopeful vibes with this summer-inclined collection of flavors, a delicious balance of fresh, tangy, and richness.

Yield: 4 to 6 Servings

Melon Shooter (see page 36)

½ lb. chopped watermelon

½ lb. cantaloupe balls

4 oz. prosciutto

Leaves from 2 sprigs of fresh mint

1 tablespoon aged balsamic vinegar

Salt and pepper, to taste

1 Divide the Melon Shooter among four vessels and place them in four different points on the board, leaving plenty of space in between them.

2 Distribute the watermelon and cantaloupe over the board.

3 Roll up the prosciutto and place it on the board, overlapping some of it with the other ingredients.

4 Sprinkle the mint over the board, lightly drizzle the balsamic vinegar over the top, season with salt and pepper, and enjoy.

MELON SHOOTER

Yield: 2 Cups
Active Time: 5 Minutes
Total Time: 5 Minutes

14 oz. chopped cantaloupe

½ teaspoon kosher salt

1 tablespoon honey

Zest and juice of 1 lime

Leaves from 2 sprigs of fresh mint

1   Place all of the ingredients in a blender and puree until smooth.

2   Taste, adjust the seasoning as necessary, and chill in the refrigerator before serving.

PICNIC BOARD

Yield: 2 to 4 Servings

1 baguette

3 oz. fruit preserves

5 oz. cured sausage, sliced

4 oz. smoked salmon

1 wedge of blue cheese

1 small wheel of goat cheese

1 wedge of brie cheese

2 oz. dip

1 oz. honey

2 oz. chocolate-covered almonds

3 oz. trail mix

2 oz. mozzarella cheese

2 oz. cornichons

This board is designed to be packed up and enjoyed outdoors by yourself and your loved ones. This means you should give considerable thought to how each item is going to be served when making your selections—softer cheeses, dips and preserves that are already in a mason jar, and pre-cut charcuterie will allow you to stop stressing about the snacks and focus on nature. And, while you can certainly bring a board along, we suggest using small plates instead and placing other items that are packaged directly on the picnic blanket to create a more intimate experience!

1   Pack all of your ingredients in glass containers or bento boxes and store them in the refrigerator so that everything stays as cool as possible.

2   Once you are at your picnic location, arrange some items on plates and some on the picnic basket itself and enjoy.

IT'S A CELEBRATION BOARD

Whether you're celebrating a milestone, expressing gratitude, or simply treating someone who's in need of a pick-me-up, this charcuterie gift basket is sure to leave a lasting impression. If you're not going to be enjoying it straight off, make sure to wrap the basket in cellophane before it gets transported.

Yield: 2 to 4 Servings

1 (750 ml) bottle of Champagne

3 wrapped artisanal cheeses

2 to 3 unopened local or homemade jams, honey, and/or dips

2 to 3 oz. cured meat

2 oz. cheese, sliced

2 oz. meat jerky

2 to 3 oz. fresh fruit

1 to 2 oz. pickled vegetables

Flowers, for decoration

1 Place the bottle of Champagne and any other items you are giving as a gift inside a basket.

2 Fill in any gaps with the artisanal cheeses and jars of jams, honey, and/or dips.

3 Thread the cured meat, cheese, meat jerky, fruit, and pickled vegetables onto skewers.

4 Make cones out of pieces of parchment paper, place the skewers in them, and add them to the basket.

5 Decorate the basket with flowers, present your gift basket, and enjoy the charcuterie skewers immediately afterward.

EASTER BOARD

Easter is a holiday that cries out for color and symbols of life, both of which are answered by the Pickled Eggs. And stow away the suggestion to use cookie cutters to shape the cheese, as it's an effective and easy way to articulate a theme on a board.

Yield: 4 to 6 Servings

4 oz. gouda cheese

2 oz. jam or fruit preserves

3 oz. Roasted Baby Beets (see page 44)

¼ oz. sprigs of fresh thyme

4 Pickled Eggs (see page 45)

4 oz. ham

2 oz. salami

3 oz. strawberries

1 oz. radishes, cut into wedges

2 oz. chocolate-coated almonds

Fresh herbs, for garnish

Edible flower blossoms, for garnish

1   Using Easter-themed cookie cutters, cut the gouda into various shapes and distribute them over a board.

2   Place the jam in a ramekin and some of the beets in another one. Place them on the board.

3   Use the sprigs of thyme to make 4 nests on the board: start by making a triangle with three small sprigs, and then repeat, rotating the triangle slightly so that the points of the second triangle overlap the center of the first triangle's edges. Repeat with one more triangle.

4   Place a Pickled Egg in each of the nests.

5   Roll up the ham and place it on the board.

6   Fill in the remaining space on the board with the salami, strawberries, radishes, remaining beets, and chocolate-coated almonds, garnish with the fresh herbs and flower blossoms, and enjoy.

ROASTED BABY BEETS

Yield: 4 Servings
Active Time: 20 Minutes
Total Time: 1 Hour and 50 Minutes

4 baby beets (about ½ lb.)

¼ cup extra-virgin olive oil, plus more to taste

Salt, to taste

4 sprigs of fresh rosemary

4 sprigs of fresh thyme

8 fresh sage leaves

1   Preheat the oven to 350°F and line a baking sheet with aluminum foil.

2   Place the beets and olive oil in a mixing bowl, season with salt, and toss to combine. Place the beets on the baking sheet, add the fresh herbs, and cover the baking sheet with aluminum foil.

3   Place the beets in the oven and roast until a knife inserted into them easily passes through to the center, about 1½ hours.

4   Remove the beets from the oven and keep them covered for 10 minutes.

5   Peel the beets and cut them to the desired size. Place them in a bowl, season with olive oil and salt, and serve.

PICKLED EGGS

Yield: 4 Eggs
Active Time: 20 Minutes
Total Time: 1 Day

1½ cups water

¾ cup rice vinegar

3 tablespoons kosher salt

½ cup plus 1 tablespoon sugar

2 tablespoons peeled and diced red beets

4 large eggs

1   Place the water, vinegar, salt, sugar, and beets in a small saucepan and bring to a gentle simmer, stirring to dissolve the salt and sugar.

2   Remove the pan from heat and let the brine cool.

3   Fill a pot with 2 quarts of water and bring to a boil.

4   Add the eggs to the water and let the water return to a boil. Once it does, set a timer and cook the eggs for 10 minutes.

5   Gently remove the eggs from the water with a strainer and run them under cold water until they are cool. You do not want to cool down the eggs in an ice bath, as the inner membrane will stick to the egg white when you peel them.

6   Gently peel the eggs, taking care to keep the egg white intact.

7   Submerge the eggs in the cooled brine and let them pickle in the refrigerator for at least 24 hours before serving.

CINCO DE MAYO BOARD

A board that provides the perfect departure point for an all-night celebration of the numerous gifts Mexican culture has given to the world.

Yield: 4 to 6 Servings

Tajín Crema (see page 49)

Chorizo (see page 48)

Blistered Shishito Peppers (see page 51)

4 oz. chicharrón (pork rinds)

2 to 3 oz. queso fresco, cubed

1 lime, cut into segments

1   Place the Tajín Crema in a bowl and place it at the top of a board.

2   Arrange the Chorizo in a line next to the Tajín Crema.

3   Place the peppers in the middle of the board and the chicharrón on the right side.

4   Fill in any gaps with the queso fresco and lime and enjoy.

Yield: 16 Patties
Active Time: 30 Minutes
Total Time: 45 Minutes

CHORIZO

2 lbs. ground pork

1 tablespoon kosher salt

1½ tablespoons ancho chile powder

1 tablespoon paprika

¼ cup finely chopped chipotle peppers in adobo

¼ teaspoon black pepper

2 teaspoons dried oregano

1 tablespoon cumin

1 tablespoon chopped garlic

1 tablespoon tequila

1 tablespoon red wine vinegar

2 tablespoons diced yellow onion

¼ teaspoon ground cloves

1 teaspoon cinnamon

½ teaspoon dried thyme

2 tablespoons extra-virgin olive oil

1   Place all of the ingredients, except for the olive oil, in the work bowl of a stand mixer fitted with the paddle attachment. Work the mixture until it is thoroughly combined, 1 to 2 minutes.

2   Cook a small piece of the mixture in the microwave until it is cooked through. Taste and adjust the seasoning as necessary. Form the mixture into 2 oz. patties.

3   Place the olive oil in a large skillet and warm it over medium heat. Working in batches, add the chorizo and cook until they are browned on both sides and the interior is 160ºF, turning them over as necessary.

4   When all of the chorizo has been cooked, serve immediately.

Yield: 3 oz.
Active Time: 5 Minutes
Total Time: 5 Minutes

⅓ cup Mexican crema

Zest and juice of 1 lime

1 tablespoon tajín

TAJÍN CREMA

1   Place all of the ingredients in a bowl and stir to combine.

2   Taste, adjust the seasoning as necessary, and serve.

BLISTERED SHISHITO PEPPERS

Yield: 4 Servings
Active Time: 10 Minutes
Total Time: 10 Minutes

2 tablespoons canola oil

½ lb. shishito peppers

½ teaspoon kosher salt

1 Warm a large cast-iron skillet over high heat until it is hot enough that a drop of water instantly evaporates on its surface.

2 Add the canola oil to the pan. Add the peppers in a single layer, making sure that all of the peppers are touching the surface. Reduce the heat to medium and cook the peppers without touching them until they start to blister, about 3 minutes.

3 Flip the peppers over and cook until the other side is blistered, about 2 minutes.

4 Remove the peppers from the pan, season with the salt, and serve.

SMOKED SALMON BOARD

A combination of refined and rustic, this is a spread that will work any time of day, in any situation, one that is guaranteed to bring people together around a table, and keep them there.

Yield: 8 to 10 Servings

Smoked Salmon (see page 55)

2 oz. Chive Crème Fraîche (see page 56)

2 oz. cucumbers, sliced

2 oz. red onion, sliced

2 tablespoons capers

1 oz. arugula

6 oz. crackers or bread

1   Place the Smoked Salmon in the center of a board.

2   Place the Chive Crème Fraîche in a small ramekin and place it on the board.

3   Arrange the remaining ingredients on the board, place a knife and a fork on the board so everyone can serve themselves, and enjoy.

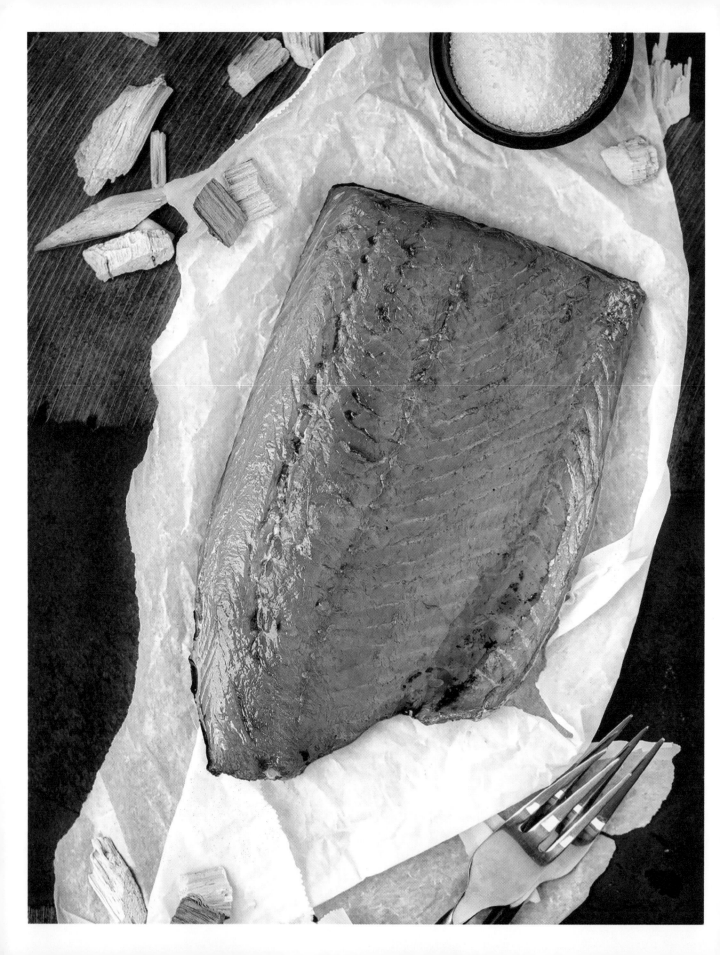

SMOKED SALMON

Yield: 8 to 10 Servings
Active Time: 25 Minutes
Total Time: 2 Days

2 tablespoons kosher salt

1 tablespoon sugar

2 lbs. skin-on salmon fillet

¼ cup fresh dill

Zest of 1 lemon

1   Place the salt and sugar in a dish and stir to combine. Set the mixture aside.

2   Place the salmon in a large container and pat it dry with a paper towel. Spread the salt-and-sugar mixture over the flesh, patting it gently to make sure it adheres.

3   Sprinkle the dill and lemon zest over the salmon and wrap it tightly with plastic wrap. Repeat with 2 more pieces of plastic wrap, making sure that no liquid will escape.

4   Chill the salmon in the refrigerator for 36 hours.

5   Remove the salmon from the refrigerator and unwrap it. Brush off the lemon zest, dill, and salt mixture and rinse it under cold water.

6   Pat the salmon dry and transfer it to a container. Chill it in the refrigerator, uncovered, for 6 to 8 hours.

7   Preheat a smoker to 250ºF.

8   Smoke the salmon until it turns a pale pink color and you see little flecks of white protein seeping out of the flesh, 30 to 40 minutes. The internal temperature should be at least 135°F.

9   Remove the salmon from the smoker and chill it in the refrigerator before serving.

CHIVE CRÈME FRAÎCHE

Yield: ½ Cup
Active Time: 5 Minutes
Total Time: 30 Minutes

½ cup crème fraîche

Zest and juice of 1 lemon

⅛ teaspoon Tabasco

⅛ teaspoon Worcestershire sauce

2 tablespoons chopped fresh chives

Salt and pepper, to taste

1   Place all of the ingredients in a bowl and stir to combine.

2   Chill the crème fraîche in the refrigerator before serving.

FRUIT & NUT BOARD

A good board for those gatherings where you are looking to keep things light, but still want to impress. While there happens to be no "charcuterie" on this board, it still features ingredients that utilize two different preservation techniques—candying and rehydrating—so we're confident it makes the cut.

Yield: 2 to 4 Servings

4 oz. brie cheese, cut into wedges

2 figs, halved

1 clementine, peeled and segmented

12 Stuffed Apricots (see page 60)

2 oz. Candied Pecans (see page 63)

2 oz. trail mix

1 Distribute the brie, figs, and clementine over a board.

2 Arrange the Stuffed Apricots on the board, fill in any gaps with the Candied Pecans and trail mix, and enjoy.

STUFFED APRICOTS

Yield: 12 Apricots
Active Time: 30 Minutes
Total Time: 35 Minutes

2 oz. plus 1 teaspoon sugar

¼ cup water

12 dried apricots

2 oz. mascarpone cheese

⅛ teaspoon cinnamon

⅛ teaspoon pure vanilla extract

Pinch of kosher salt

2 tablespoons crushed pistachios

1   Place 2 oz. of sugar and the water in a small saucepan and bring it to a simmer, stirring to dissolve the sugar.

2   Add the apricots to the syrup and reduce the heat so that the syrup gently simmers. Cook for 1 minute, turn off the heat, and let the apricots rest in the syrup as it cools.

3   Place the mascarpone, cinnamon, vanilla, salt, and remaining sugar in the work bowl of a stand mixer fitted with the whisk attachment and whip until the mixture is light and airy. Taste, adjust the seasoning as necessary, and place the mascarpone cream in a piping bag fitted with a plain tip.

4   Insert your finger into the centers of the rehydrated apricots and create a small hole.

5   Fill the apricots with the mascarpone cream, making sure some comes out the top.

6   Place the pistachios in a small dish and dip the stuffed apricots into them, making sure the mascarpone cream is coated. Serve immediately.

CANDIED PECANS

Yield: 8 Servings
Active Time: 20 Minutes
Total Time: 2 Hours and 15 Minutes

3 egg whites

½ teaspoon pure vanilla extract

1 teaspoon cinnamon

⅓ cup sugar

¾ lb. pecans

1 teaspoon kosher salt

1. Preheat the oven to 225°F. Line a baking sheet with a Silpat mat and coat it with nonstick cooking spray.

2. Place the egg whites in the work bowl of a stand mixer fitted with the whisk attachment. Make sure that the bowl is very clean and that none of the egg yolks got in with the egg whites, as grease and fats from the egg yolk make the whites more difficult to whip.

3. Add the vanilla and cinnamon to the egg whites and begin whipping the mixture at low speed for 10 seconds.

4. Raise the speed to medium-high and whip until the egg whites become frothy and start to increase in volume. Slowly stream in the sugar and whip until the egg whites hold soft peaks and are smooth and glossy.

5. Remove the work bowl from the stand mixer and gently add the pecans to the whipped egg whites. Fold to combine. Spread the pecans on the baking sheet in an even layer and season them with salt. Place the pecans in the oven and bake for 30 minutes.

6. Remove the pecans from the oven and use a rubber spatula to lift the pecans from the pan and break them up. Once all of the large clumps are broken up, spread the pecans on the sheet in an even layer, return them to the oven, and bake for another 30 minutes.

7. Remove the pecans from the oven and use a rubber spatula to lift the pecans from the pan and break them up. Once all of the large clumps are broken up, spread the pecans on the sheet in an even layer, return them to the oven, and bake until they are completely dry, about 30 minutes.

8. Remove the pecans from the oven and let them cool completely before serving or storing in an airtight container.

SUMMER

With all that warmth and sunshine, everyone knows that summer is the time to have fun. But the incredible excitement that the season fosters has a tendency to stretch us all too thin. In an attempt to keep you from getting sucked up in that frenzy, we've curated a series of spreads that make it easy to take a step back. And, thanks to a number of preparations that don't require the use of an oven or a stove, keeping your cool in your host role won't be a problem.

One of the very best things about summer is the potential for a normal, low-key gathering to stretch out into the early evening and night, powered by the momentum that good people and beautiful weather can provide. We've composed these boards with these magical occasions in mind, selecting recipes that provide the perfect launching pad for such get-togethers.

SUMMERTIME IS HERE BOARD

The long-awaited arrival of summer cries out for smoke and comforting foods that you can enjoy while kicking it with friends, and this board, which is a mashup of a traditional German smoked beef board and Buffalo's beloved beef on weck sandwich, fits the bill.

Yield: 4 to 6 Servings

1½ lbs. Smoked Beef (see page 68)

¾ lb. Pickled Cabbage (see page 85)

¾ lb. potato salad

Country Mustard (see page 121)

6 oz. Bread & Butter Pickles (see page 71)

Kimmelweck Rolls (see page 69)

1 Select a large board that gives plenty of space for all of the ingredients. Place the Smoked Beef on the board, slicing about three-quarters of it.

2 Place the cabbage, potato salad, mustard, and pickles on the side of the Smoked Beef.

3 Stack the rolls in front of the Smoked Beef and enjoy.

Yield: 12 Servings
Active Time: 15 Minutes
Total Time: 3 Days

16 cups water

1½ cups kosher salt

6 teaspoons pink curing salt #1

1 cup sugar

½ cup brown sugar

1 tablespoon Pickling Spice (see page 245)

4 garlic cloves, smashed

2 oz. fresh rosemary

2 oz. fresh thyme

2 oz. fresh sage

5 lbs. beef brisket or chuck roast

¼ cup cracked black peppercorns

Beef stock, as needed

SMOKED BEEF

1   Place the water, salts, sugars, Pickling Spice, and garlic in a stockpot and bring to a simmer, stirring to dissolve the salts and sugars.

2   Add the rosemary, thyme, and sage and remove the pan from heat. Let the brine cool completely.

3   Place the beef in the brine and weigh it down to ensure that it stays fully submerged. Brine the beef in the refrigerator for 3 days.

4   Preheat your smoker to 200ºF.

5   Remove the beef from the brine, rinse it with cold water, and pat it dry. Press the pepper into it so that the pepper will form a crust as the beef cooks.

6   Place the beef in the smoker and smoke until it has an internal temperature between 120°F to 130°F. Remove the beef from the smoker, cover it loosely with aluminum foil, and let it cool completely. Transfer the beef to the refrigerator until it is chilled.

7   Cut the beef into thin slices. Add some stock to a saucepan and bring it to a simmer.

8   Turn off the heat under the saucepan and add the beef to the stock. Let it sit until it has warmed and then serve.

KIMMELWECK ROLLS

Yield: 6 Rolls
Active Time: 15 Minutes
Total Time: 3 Hours and 45 Minutes

⅓ oz. (10 g) active dry yeast

½ oz. (16 g) sugar

5⅓ oz. (150 g) lukewarm water (90°F)

9.2 oz. (260 g) bread flour

3½ oz. (100 g) whole wheat flour

1 whole egg

⅓ oz. (10 g) kosher salt

½ oz. (15 g) honey

1 oz. (34 g) extra-virgin olive oil, plus more as needed

1 oz. (30 g) buttermilk, plus more for topping

¾ oz. (25 g) caraway seeds, plus more for topping

Coarse sea salt, for topping

1   Place the yeast, sugar, and water in the work bowl of a stand mixer fitted with the dough hook and gently stir to combine. Let the mixture sit until it starts to foam, about 10 minutes.

2   Place the flours, egg, salt, honey, olive oil, and buttermilk in a mixing bowl and stir to combine. Add the mixture to the work bowl and knead at medium speed until the mixture comes together as a dough.

3   Add the caraway seeds and knead at a medium-low speed until the dough is smooth and comes away easily from the sides of the work bowl, 6 to 8 minutes.

4   Coat a clean bowl with olive oil, place the dough in it, and cover the bowl loosely with plastic wrap. Place the bowl in a naturally warm place until the dough has doubled in size, about 1 hour.

5   Gently press down on the dough to release some of the gasses. Divide the dough into 3½ oz. pieces and form them into balls.

6   Coat a baking sheet with olive oil and place the balls on it. Cover them loosely with plastic wrap and let them rest until they have tripled in size, about 2 hours.

7   Preheat the oven to 425°F. Gently brush the tops of the rolls with buttermilk and sprinkle caraway seeds and coarse sea salt over them.

8   Place the rolls in the oven and bake until they are golden brown, 20 to 22 minutes, rotating the pan halfway through.

9   Remove the rolls from the oven and let them cool slightly before serving.

BREAD & BUTTER PICKLES

Yield: 1 Pint
Active Time: 25 Minutes
Total Time: 24 Hours

1½ cups water

¾ cup rice vinegar

3 tablespoons kosher salt

½ cup plus 2 tablespoons sugar

1 large cucumber

4 large sprigs of fresh dill

3 garlic cloves, smashed

1   Place the water, vinegar, salt, and sugar in a small saucepan and bring it to a gentle simmer, stirring to dissolve the salt and sugar.

2   Fit a mandoline with a corrugated blade to create ridges in your pickles and slice the cucumber into circles with your desired thickness.

3   Place the cucumber in a mason jar and add the dill and garlic.

4   Pour the brine into the mason jar and gently stir. Place a lid on the jar, but do not fully tighten it. Chill the pickles in the refrigerator overnight before serving.

CHOOSE YOUR OWN ADVENTURE BOARD

This spread is a great example of how easily you can craft a memorable board: deconstruct a universally loved preparation (the BLT), put a unique, delicious spin on 1 or 2 of the elements (Herb Mayo, Spicy Maple Bacon), and give people the freedom to tailor bites to their own palates.

Yield: 4 to 6 Servings

¼ cup Herb Mayo (see page 76)

16 large leaves of Bibb lettuce

8 slices of bread, toasted

16 slices of Spicy Maple Bacon (see page 75), halved

2 large heirloom tomatoes, sliced

1   Place the Herb Mayo in a bowl and place it on one side of the board, near the edge.

2   Arrange the lettuce, bread, bacon, and tomatoes around the bowl and enjoy.

SPICY MAPLE BACON

Yield: 12 Servings
Active Time: 25 Minutes
Total Time: 8½ Days

2½ lb. slab of pork belly

3 tablespoons Standard Cure (see page 246)

¼ teaspoon red pepper flakes

1½ tablespoons maple syrup, plus more to taste

1. Place the pork belly in a baking pan that fits securely around it. Rub the Standard Cure all over the surface.

2. Sprinkle the red pepper flakes over the pork belly and brush it with the maple syrup.

3. Cover the pork belly with plastic wrap, transfer it to the refrigerator, and let it cure for 7 days, turning it over every other day.

4. Place a wire rack in a rimmed baking pan. Remove the pork belly from the refrigerator and rinse it under cold water. Pat it dry, place it on the wire rack, and let it dry out in the refrigerator for 24 hours.

5. Preheat a smoker to 200°F to 250°F.

6. If you prefer your bacon to be on the sweeter side, brush the pork belly with additional maple syrup. Place it in the smoker and smoke it until it reaches an internal temperature of 150°F, 2½ hours to 3 hours.

7. Remove the bacon from the smoker and let it cool before slicing them into ⅛-inch-thick strips, slicing against the grain.

8. Cook the bacon in a pan on the stovetop or in the oven at 350°F until it reaches your desired level of doneness and enjoy.

Yield: ½ Cup
Active Time: 5 Minutes
Total Time: 5 Minutes

½ cup mayonnaise

1 tablespoon chopped fresh parsley

1 tablespoon chopped fresh chives

1 teaspoon chopped fresh dill

¼ teaspoon chopped fresh thyme

2 garlic cloves, minced

1 tablespoon buttermilk

2 dashes of Tabasco

2 dashes of Worcestershire sauce

2 pinches of black pepper

¼ teaspoon kosher salt

HERB MAYO

1   Place all of the ingredients in a bowl and stir until thoroughly combined.

2   Taste, adjust the seasoning as necessary, and use as desired.

BACKYARD BBQ BOARD

Barbecue joints are great, but any time spent out on the road, away from the comforts of home during the summer, is a loss. Fire up the smoker and keep things simple with this flavorful collection of bespoke bites.

Yield: 6 to 8 Servings

2 lbs. Pulled Pork (see page 80)

8 brioche buns

1 rack of Pork Ribs (see page 84)

½ cup BBQ sauce

1 lb. coleslaw

1   Place the Pulled Pork in the middle of the board and the brioche buns next to it.

2   Place the Pork Ribs close to the pulled pork and generously lather each with BBQ sauce.

3   Place the coleslaw in a small bowl and place it on the opposite side of the board. Place any remaining BBQ sauce in a ramekin, place it beside the coleslaw, and enjoy.

Yield: 16 Servings
Active Time: 15 Minutes
Total Time: 32 Hours

5 to 6 lb. boneless pork shoulder

Salt and pepper, to taste

½ to ¾ cup BBQ Rub (see page 242)

PULLED PORK

1   The day before you plan on smoking the pork, remove it from the refrigerator and season it generously with salt and pepper. Don't be afraid to use a good amount of salt, because you want it to penetrate deeply into the pork.

2   Generously coat the pork shoulder with the rub and cover it tightly with plastic wrap. Let the pork shoulder chill in the refrigerator overnight.

3   About 6 hours before smoking, place a wire rack in a rimmed baking sheet. Take the pork out of the refrigerator and unwrap it. Place it on the wire rack and place it back in the refrigerator, uncovered. During this step, the pork will form a sticky layer on the outside that will allow smoke to adhere to the pork at a higher rate and give you a beautiful, deep smoke ring.

4   About 1 hour before you are planning to put the pork on the smoker, preheat the smoker to 250°F.

5   Place the pork in the smoker and place a drip pan underneath it to catch the drippings.

6   Smoke the pork for 3 to 4 hours until it develops a nice crust, checking on it every hour.

7   Preheat the oven to 275°F. Remove the pork from the smoker and place it in a Dutch oven. Cover the pot, place it in the oven, and cook until the pork has an internal temperature of 185°F, 2 to 3 hours.

8   Remove the pork from the oven and let it rest for 30 minutes before shredding it with two forks and serving.

FOURTH OF JULY BOARD

The day that the entire season points toward needs a board that captures its spirit. Flashes of red, white, and blue do just that, and supply the refreshing quality required to balance out the richness of the Pork Ribs.

Yield: 6 to 8 Servings

Pork Ribs (see page 84)

4 oz. Pickled Cabbage (see page 85)

½ lb. potato salad

8 slices of Watermelon Fruit Salad (see page 86)

4 oz. fresh strawberries, hulled and quartered

4 oz. bananas, sliced

3 oz. fresh blueberries

1   Place the Pork Ribs on one side of a large board, stacking the ribs on top of one another.

2   Place the Pickled Cabbage in a small bowl and the potato salad in another one. Place the bowls on opposite sides of the board.

3   Place the Watermelon Fruit Salad between the two bowls.

4   Place the strawberries in a line beside the ribs. Arrange the bananas next to the strawberries and the blueberries beside the bananas, forming a red, white, and blue display.

FOURTH OF JULY BOARD, SEE PAGE 81

Yield: 8 Servings
Active Time: 25 Minutes
Total Time: 29 Hours

2 racks of baby back pork ribs

Salt and pepper, to taste

½ cup BBQ Rub (see page 242)

BBQ sauce, for coating and for serving

PORK RIBS

1 The day before you plan on smoking the ribs, remove them from the refrigerator and season them generously with salt and pepper. Don't be afraid to use a good amount of salt, because you want it to penetrate deeply into the pork.

2 Generously coat the ribs with the rub and cover them tightly with plastic wrap. Let the ribs chill in the refrigerator overnight.

3 Preheat a smoker to 250ºF.

4 Place the ribs in the smoker and smoke them until they are tender but not falling apart, about 4 hours. You should be able to separate the meat from the bones, but it should still have some resistance.

5 If desired, brush the ribs with BBQ sauce and smoke them for another 10 to 15 minutes.

6 Remove the ribs from the smoker, cut them into the desired sizes, and serve with BBQ sauce.

PICKLED CABBAGE

Yield: 8 Cups
Active Time: 30 Minutes
Total Time: 35 Minutes

3 cups water

1½ cups apple cider vinegar

1¼ cups sugar

6 tablespoons kosher salt

1 small head of green cabbage, cored and sliced thin

1 small yellow onion, julienned

1 tablespoon mustard seeds

1　Place the water, vinegar, sugar, and salt in a small saucepan and bring to a gentle simmer, stirring to dissolve the sugar and salt.

2　Place the cabbage and onion in a bowl and toss to combine. Transfer the mixture to mason jars and divide the mustard seeds among them.

3　Pour the brine into the mason jars and gently stir.

4　Place a lid on each jar, but do not fully tighten it. Chill the pickled cabbage in the refrigerator overnight before serving.

WATERMELON FRUIT SALAD

Yield: 8 Servings

Active Time: 30 Minutes

Total Time: 4 Hours

4 lb. seedless watermelon

1¼ lbs. mixed fruit, cut for a fruit salad

1¼ cups watermelon juice

¾ oz. powdered gelatin

1¼ cups water

1 oz. sugar

2 pinches of kosher salt

1   Place the watermelon on a cutting board and cut the top of it off so that you can access the inside. Reserve the top of the watermelon and set it aside.

2   Scoop out the inside of the watermelon, being sure not to penetrate either the sides or the bottom of the melon. Once all of the watermelon has been scooped out, place the emptied-out rind upside down and let it drain.

3   Transfer 1¼ cups of watermelon to a blender and puree until it is smooth. Dice the remaining watermelon and add it to your mixture of fruit.

4   Transfer the mixed fruit to your drained watermelon, making sure the watermelon is full, but that you can still place the top back on it so that it sits flush.

5   Add the gelatin to the watermelon juice and whisk vigorously until it has been incorporated. Let the mixture sit for 5 minutes.

6   Place the water in a medium saucepan and bring it to a boil. Add the sugar and salt and then slowly stream the boiling water into the watermelon juice-and-gelatin mixture. Stir vigorously until all of the clumps of gelatin have dissolved and you are left with one homogenous liquid. If all of the gelatin does not dissolve, gently heat the mixture while stirring until all of the clumps have dissolved. Let the watermelon gelatin cool to room temperature.

7   Carefully pour the watermelon gelatin over the fruit inside the watermelon. Immediately place the top back on the watermelon, place it in the refrigerator, and chill it until the gelatin is fully set, about 3 hours.

8   To serve, remove the top from the watermelon and slice the melon in half lengthwise. Slice each half into 4 long pieces and then slice these into 1-inch-thick pieces. Serve chilled.

ON THE GO BOARDS

While the summer is a lot of fun, it's also a season where it seems like we're always on the go. These "boards" are well suited to this way of life, providing comfort, energy, and allowing you to linger a little longer in those picturesque spots you've journeyed to. The key to the perfect travel charcuterie "board" is to have 5 components: fresh fruit, charcuterie, cheeses, something salty like olives, and something sweet like chocolate. This will ensure that you have the most balanced board that will satisfy all cravings.

Yield: 4 Servings

24 crackers

2 oz. cheese, small slices

2 oz. fresh fruit

2 oz. olives

2 oz. chocolate-covered almonds

4 oz. cured meat

2 oz. raisins or other dried fruit

1 Divide the crackers among your chosen containers.

2 Top with the cheese, stack the remaining ingredients on top, and enjoy.

SUMMER BREEZE BOARD

Step into the bright and breezy spirit of summer with this refreshing spread, which is all about enjoying the simple but pleasant sensations that summer provides.

Yield: 4 to 6 Servings

4 oz. mortadella, sliced

3 oz. feta cheese

½ lb. chopped fresh watermelon

2 oz. Pickled Watermelon Rind (see page 93)

1 oz. shelled pistachios

Leaves from 5 sprigs of fresh mint

Salt and pepper, to taste

1   Fold the slices of mortadella in half or in quarters and distribute them on the board.

2   Cut the feta into long rectangles and arrange them and the fresh watermelon on the board.

3   Distribute the pickled watermelon over the board and then fill in any gaps with pistachios.

4   Sprinkle the mint over everything, season with salt and pepper, and enjoy.

PICKLED WATERMELON RIND

Yield: 1 Quart
Active Time: 25 Minutes
Total Time: 24 Hours

1½ cups water

¾ cup Champagne vinegar

3 tablespoons kosher salt

¾ cup sugar

1 lb. watermelon rinds, cut into strips

3 whole cloves

Zest and juice of 1 lemon

1 Place the water, vinegar, salt, and sugar in a small saucepan and bring to a gentle simmer, stirring to dissolve the salt and sugar.

2 Place the watermelon rinds, cloves, lemon zest, and lemon juice in a large mason jar.

3 Pour the brine into the mason jar and gently stir.

4 Place a lid on the jar, but do not fully tighten it. Chill the pickled watermelon rind in the refrigerator overnight before serving.

NATIONAL ICE CREAM DAY BOARD

Every July 21 is a celebration of the ultimate treat, ice cream. And while it will be tempting to eat ice cream all day, it's also a good idea to get something other than sugar in your system. This inventive board honors the day, but provides some much needed protein, and it's also a well-balanced collection of tastes and textures, as the tartare almost melts in your mouth, the cones add a satisfying crunch and sweetness, and the puffed rice provides an irresistible nuttiness.

Yield: 6 to 8 Servings

Tuna Tartare (see page 97)

Wonton Cones (see page 98)

¼ cup Forbidden Black Rice Sprinkles (see page 101)

1   Spoon the Tuna Tartare into the Wonton Cones, making sure that some of the tuna goes into the cones and some sits on top.

2   Sprinkle the Forbidden Black Rice Sprinkles on top of the cones, place them in an ice cream cone holder, and enjoy.

¼ cup extra-virgin olive oil

2 tablespoons soy sauce

1 tablespoon sweet soy sauce

1 tablespoon honey

1 tablespoon hoisin

2 tablespoons sesame oil

½ teaspoon grated fresh ginger

1 tablespoon grated fresh lemongrass

2 tablespoons rice vinegar

Zest and juice of 1 lime

¼ teaspoon gochujang

3 oz. sushi-grade tuna, diced into ¼-inch cubes

3 oz. ripe mango, diced into ¼-inch cubes

3 oz. avocado, diced into ¼-inch cubes

2 tablespoons chopped scallion

TUNA TARTARE

1   Place all of the ingredients, except for the tuna, mango, avocado, and scallion, in a blender and puree until smooth. Taste and adjust the seasoning as necessary.

2   Place the tuna, mango, and avocado in a bowl, add ¼ cup of the marinade, and toss to coat. Let the tuna tartare marinate for 15 minutes.

3   Add the scallion, toss to combine, and serve.

WONTON CONES

Yield: 16 Cones
Active Time: 20 Minutes
Total Time: 30 Minutes

4 cups canola oil

16 Hong Kong–style wonton wrappers

1 Place the canola oil in a small pot and warm it to 350°F.

2 Place a 3⅓-inch stainless steel baking cone at the edge of a wonton wrapper and roll the wrapper up around the cone. Place the wrapper, still wrapped around the cone, into another baking cone so that it maintains its shape while frying.

3 Gently slip the wrapper, sandwiched between the baking cones, into the hot oil and cook until the cone is golden brown, about 2 minutes.

4 Remove the cone from the oil, strain off any excess oil, and let the wonton cool briefly before removing it from the baking cones. Repeat with the remaining wonton wrappers.

FORBIDDEN BLACK RICE SPRINKLES

Yield: 12 Servings
Active Time: 20 Minutes
Total Time: 20 Minutes

2 cups canola oil

1 oz. forbidden black rice

¼ teaspoon kosher salt

1   Before puffing the rice, it is important to know that it will bubble rapidly and expand. Make sure that you do not add too much rice at once and that your pot is big enough to accommodate the expansion.

2   Place the canola oil in a Dutch oven and warm it to 425°F.

3   Line a baking sheet with paper towels and place it beside the stove. Place a spider strainer beside the stove as well.

4   Working in batches, gently slip the rice into the hot oil and fry it for 20 to 30 seconds, until all of the kernels have puffed up. Remove the puffed rice with the strainer and place it on the paper towel–lined baking sheet to drain.

5   Season the puffed rice with salt and serve.

IT'S PEACH SEASON BOARD

As peach season is all too brief, it's important to find as many ways as you can to make the most of it. This board does just that, providing three peach-centered preparations that highlight its unique flavor and versatility. And, as a peach's sweetness calls for something creamy and something salty, the burrata and country ham are natural partners.

Yield: 2 to 4 Servings

4 oz. burrata, cut into four pieces

2 oz. Lavender & Peach Jam (see page 106)

4 oz. country ham, sliced thin

2 Grilled Peaches (see page 104), sliced

3 oz. Preserved Peaches (see page 107)

Fresh basil, for garnish

Fresh lavender, for garnish

Marigolds, for garnish

Balsamic vinegar, for garnish

1 Distribute the pieces of burrata around a board, ensuring that there is plenty of space between them.

2 Place the Lavender & Peach Jam in a ramekin and place it on the board. Fold and/or twist the country ham and scatter it over the board.

3 Distribute the Grilled Peaches and Preserved Peaches over the board, overlapping these with the ham.

4 Garnish with basil, lavender, and marigolds, drizzle balsamic vinegar over everything, and enjoy.

GRILLED PEACHES

Yield: 4 Servings
Active Time: 20 Minutes
Total Time: 30 Minutes

2 ripe peaches, halved and pitted

¼ teaspoon cinnamon

2 pinches of kosher salt

2 teaspoons honey

1 tablespoon extra-virgin olive oil

1 Prepare a gas or charcoal grill for medium heat (about 400°F).

2 Season the cut sides of the peaches with the cinnamon and salt. Brush the cut sides with honey and olive oil.

3 Place the peaches, cut side down, on the grill and cook until the fruit has started to soften and grill marks are present, 4 to 5 minutes. The peaches should not stick to the grill when moved if they are ready.

4 Either remove the peaches from the grill and enjoy, or flip them over and continue cooking the peaches for another 2 minutes if a softer texture and stronger charred flavor are desired.

LAVENDER & PEACH JAM

Yield: 4 Cups
Active Time: 25 Minutes
Total Time: 2 Hours and 40 Minutes

½ cup water

¼ cup fresh lavender

Zest and juice of 2 lemons

4 cups chopped peaches

3 cups sugar

1½ teaspoons kosher salt

1 Place the water in a small saucepan and bring it to a simmer. Add the lavender and lemon zest and simmer for 4 minutes.

2 Remove the pan from heat and let the lavender and lemon zest steep for 6 minutes.

3 Place the peaches, lemon juice, sugar, and salt in a large pot.

4 Strain the lavender tea into the pot and discard the lavender and lemon zest.

5 Bring the mixture to a gentle simmer, reduce the heat to low, and cook for 2 hours, stirring occasionally to ensure that nothing sticks to the sides or bottom of the pot.

6 Remove the pan from heat and let the jam cool for 15 minutes.

7 Transfer the jam to a blender and puree until it is velvety smooth. Let the jam cool completely before serving.

PRESERVED PEACHES

Yield: 2 Cups
Active Time: 20 Minutes
Total Time: 24 Hours

1 cup sugar

1 cup water

1 small knob of fresh ginger, peeled and roughly chopped

3 peaches, pitted and cut into wedges

3 whole cloves

½ cinnamon stick

1 Place the sugar and water in a small pot and bring to a boil, stirring to dissolve the sugar. Reduce the heat so that the syrup gently simmers and add the ginger.

2 Cook the ginger for 2 minutes. Add the peaches and cook for 1 minute.

3 Remove the pan from heat, add the cloves and cinnamon stick, and let the mixture cool to room temperature before transferring to a mason jar and refrigerating.

4 Chill the peaches in the refrigerator overnight before serving.

BIRTHDAY BOARD

Yes, people have birthdays all year long. But we've decided to situate this board in the summer because those who were born in June, July, and August had to spend their childhoods suffering through everyone else getting their special day celebrated in school, and they deserve a little something to ease the pain.

Yield: 2 to 4 Servings

4 oz. cheese

6 oz. charcuterie

3 oz. fresh fruit

3 oz. dried fruit

3 oz. nuts

½ lb. birthday person's favorite snacks

1 Cut along the edges of a papier mâché letter with an X-ACTO knife. Pull off the top of the cut side and remove any cardboard filler, making sure the number is hollow inside.

2 Clean the edges, tearing off the little stray bits. Fill the inside of the letter with either tissue paper or parchment paper.

3 Arrange the cheese and charcuterie on top of the paper. Fill in any gaps with the fruit, nuts, and snacks, arrange birthday-related decorations around the board, and enjoy.

BEACH HOUSE BOARD

Sure, the ocean is beautiful and naps on the beach are delightful. But foodies know that the best part of being by the ocean is the access to fresh seafood. Break this spread out while you're on vaca by the shore, and create an unforgettable day.

Yield: 4 to 6 Servings

½ lb. Beet-Cured Salmon (see page 112)

4 oz. Smoked Salmon Rillette (see page 115)

18 to 24 shrimp chips

Nasturtiums, for garnish

1   Place slices of Beet-Cured Salmon in the middle of a board, overlapping the slices.

2   Divide the rillette among two ramekins and place them on opposite sides of the Beet-Cured Salmon.

3   Distribute the shrimp chips around the board, garnish with nasturtiums, and enjoy.

BEET-CURED SALMON

Yield: 8 Servings
Active Time: 30 Minutes
Total Time: 3 Days

4 oz. sugar

3 oz. kosher salt

½ lb. red beets, peeled and sliced thin

2 lemon peels, cut into strips

1 lb. salmon fillet, skin and pin bones removed

1. Select a container that will allow the salmon to lay flat, but is still snug around it. You don't want there to be much room because the salmon will leach out water as it cures, and you want the resulting brine to be in close contact with the salmon.

2. Place the sugar and salt in a bowl and stir to combine.

3. Arrange half of the beets in an even layer in the bottom of the container, making sure that they are covering the area where the salmon will be laid.

4. Top the beets with half of the lemon peels.

5. Sprinkle half of the sugar-and-salt mixture over the beets and lay the salmon on top. Sprinkle the sugar-and-salt mixture over the salmon and arrange the remaining beets and lemon zest on top. Place plastic wrap directly on the surface.

6. Place a pan on top of the salmon and place a weight (canned foods work well) on top of that pan in order to gently press down on the salmon.

7. Transfer the salmon to the refrigerator and let it cure for 72 hours.

8. Remove the salmon from the container, rinse it under cold water, and pat it dry. The salmon should have turned a subtle purple color and should be firm to the touch.

9. To serve, slice the salmon as thin as possible.

SMOKED SALMON RILLETTE

Yield: 8 Servings
Active Time: 10 Minutes
Total Time: 10 Minutes

½ lb. cream cheese, softened

1 tablespoon caper brine

½ lb. Smoked Salmon (see page 55)

2 tablespoons drained capers

2 tablespoons chopped chives

Salt, to taste

1 Place the cream cheese in the work bowl of a stand mixer fitted with the paddle attachment, add the caper brine, and beat until the mixture is light and airy, about 2 minutes.

2 Add the Smoked Salmon, capers, and chives and beat on low until everything is thoroughly combined, scraping down the work bowl as needed.

3 Season the rillette with salt and serve.

FALL

Fall is a time to slow down and reflect on the good times had in the recent past and the celebrations to come. Since there is a greater tendency to take it easy when autumn arrives, and the crisp air and vibrant leaves frame each day in splendor, it is the perfect season to spoil your loved ones with a decadent spread. Don't worry about going overboard—a full stomach is all the more reason to get out in the glorious light and go for a long walk.

But fall is also a time when a tightly bunched group of holidays and the increasingly dwindling sunlight can wear us down. If you get going in the season and feel like that's going to be the case, these boards provide some shelter from the storm, being filling enough to reduce your load in the kitchen and enjoyable enough to keep everyone at the table, laughing and talking.

STICK TO TRADITION BOARD

Fall marks the return to normalcy, making it a good time to turn to this board, which is filled with old standbys.

Yield: 8 to 10 Servings

1 lb. gourmet cheese (sharp cheddar cheese, aged gouda, brie)

1 lb. cured meats (prosciutto, soppressata, Genoa salami)

4 oz. pickled vegetables

2 oz. Country Mustard (see page 121)

2 oz. fruit spread or honey

Crackers, as desired

Bread, sliced, as desired

4 oz. dried fruit (apricots, cranberries)

1 Arrange the cheeses on the board, with the two largest pieces opposite of each other and the smaller slices in a neat row on the other two corners.

2 Twist the cured meats and place them near the cheeses.

3 Place the pickled vegetables in a ramekin and the Country Mustard in another one. Place the ramekins on opposite sides of the board.

4 Arrange crackers on one side of the board. Distribute bread over the entire board.

5 Fill in any gaps with dried fruit and enjoy.

COUNTRY MUSTARD

Yield: ½ Cup
Active Time: 20 Minutes
Total Time: 30 Minutes

3 tablespoons mustard seeds

½ teaspoon turmeric

¼ cup beer

1 tablespoon apple cider vinegar

1 tablespoon honey

¼ cup dry mustard

1 teaspoon kosher salt

1 teaspoon chopped fresh rosemary

1 tablespoon chopped fresh thyme

1 Place the mustard seeds and turmeric in a saucepan and warm over medium-low heat until the mixture is fragrant, shaking the pan frequently.

2 Add the beer, vinegar, and honey and bring the mixture to a simmer. Reduce the heat to low and whisk in the dry mustard and salt. Cook until most of the liquid has evaporated and the consistency is to your liking, about 5 minutes, stirring occasionally.

3 Transfer the mustard from the pan to a bowl and stir in the chopped rosemary and thyme. Let the mustard cool completely before serving.

LA DOLCE VITA BOARD

Yield: 4 to 6 Servings

6 to 8 oz. burrata, halved

4 oz. marinated olives

4 oz. pickled peppers

4 oz. marinated artichokes

4 oz. Genoa salami

4 oz. prosciutto

Crackers, sliced, as desired

Focaccia or ciabatta, sliced, as desired

4 oz. pepperoni

4 oz. ciliegine (miniature balls of mozzarella cheese)

2 oz. Garlic Confit (see page 241)

Fresh Italian flat-leaf parsley, for garnish

Fresh thyme, for garnish

Fresh basil, for garnish

Fresh oregano, for garnish

A board that celebrates the Italian flavors that have become famed across the globe. The great thing about curating this spread is that you can make it different every time by adding different elements such as Pesto (see page 155), giardiniera, or mostarda, and/or other classic Italian preparations.

1   Place the burrata on two opposite sides of the board.

2   Place the olives in a ramekin and the pickled peppers in another. Place the two ramekins on opposite sides of the board from one another, and diagonal to the burrata.

3   Place the artichokes in the center of the board, against one piece of burrata. Fold the salami and place it beside the other piece of burrata.

4   Twist the prosciutto and place it next to one piece of burrata.

5   Arrange crackers and bread around the edges of the board.

6   Fold the pepperoni in half and place some slices next to the ramekins.

7   Fill in any gaps with the mozzarella balls and Garlic Confit, garnish with the fresh herbs, and enjoy.

BACK TO SCHOOL BOARD

Though it is hard to feel nostalgic for the return to school that followed the glory of summer vacation, we all feel a slight pang at the mention of the treats of our youth. This board scratches that itch, using the inimitable Lunchable as inspiration and elevating it just enough, providing a variety of flavors, textures, and options. The amounts here are for a single serving, but can easily be adjusted for however many mouths you have to feed.

Yield: 1 Serving

4 oz. turkey or ham, sliced

2 oz. aged cheddar cheese

2 oz. Ritz crackers

2 oz. dried fruit

2 oz. cookies

1   Create as many individual snack plates as desired, placing paper plates or pieces of parchment paper over a large board.

2   On each "plate," place an even amount of turkey or ham, cheddar, crackers, dried fruit, and cookies.

COCKTAIL HOUR BOARD

It's always good to have an array of snacks on hand when cocktail hour arrives. Not only does it help you keep an even keel, it provides a great opportunity to balance flavors and experiment with inventive pairings.

Yield: 4 Servings

1 lb. Bar Nuts (see page 129)

4 oz. cheese, sliced

4 oz. salami, sliced

4 oz. crackers

2 oz. cornichons

2 Hibiscus Sours (see page 130), for serving

2 Cucumber & Mint Gin Rickeys (see page 133), for serving

1   Divide the Bar Nuts among two small ramekins and place them near the middle of the board but on opposite sides, making sure to leave plenty of space between them.

2   Arrange half of the cheese around one side of one ramekin. Arrange the remaining cheese around the opposite side of the other ramekin. The cheese slices should resemble falling dominoes.

3   Fold a piece of salami in half and then fold it in half again. Place it in the top left corner of the board. Repeat with the remaining salami, making sure you go around the ramekins, and end at about the middle of the board. The folded salami should resemble an accordion.

4   Arrange the crackers in the empty spaces on the board. Fill in any gaps with cornichons and any remaining Bar Nuts, serve with the cocktails, and enjoy.

Yield: 3½ Cups
Active Time: 30 Minutes
Total Time: 40 Minutes

3 oz. pecans

3 oz. almonds

3 oz. shelled pistachios

3 oz. cashews

3 oz. peanuts

6 oz. dried pineapple, cut into bite-sized pieces

1½ teaspoons kosher salt

2 teaspoons granulated garlic

2 teaspoons granulated onion

2 teaspoons paprika

2 teaspoons chili powder

¼ teaspoon cayenne pepper

4 teaspoons sugar

6 tablespoons unsalted butter

BAR NUTS

1 Preheat the oven to 350°F.

2 Spread the nuts in an even layer on a baking sheet, place them in the oven, and toast until they are lightly golden brown, about 6 minutes.

3 Remove the nuts from the oven, transfer them to a large bowl, and add the pineapple. Toss to combine and set the nuts aside.

4 Place all of the remaining ingredients, except for the butter, in a bowl and whisk to combine. Set the mixture aside.

5 Place the butter in a small skillet and melt it over medium heat. Cook until the butter starts to turn a light brown and gives off a nutty aroma, swirling the pan occasionally.

6 Pour the brown butter over the nuts and toss to coat. Add the spice mixture and toss to combine.

7 Taste, adjust the seasoning as necessary, and let the nuts cool completely. Use as desired and store in an airtight container.

HIBISCUS SOUR

Yield: 1 Drink
Active Time: 2 Minutes
Total Time: 2 Minutes

2 oz. reposado tequila

¾ oz. hibiscus liqueur

¾ oz. agave nectar

¾ oz. fresh lime juice

2 pinches of kosher salt

1 egg white

2 dashes of Angostura Bitters, for garnish

1. Place all of the ingredients, except for the garnish, in a cocktail shaker containing no ice and dry shake for 15 seconds.

2. Add ice to the cocktail shaker and shake until chilled.

3. Strain into a coupe, garnish with the Angostura bitters, swirling them with a toothpick, and enjoy.

CUCUMBER & MINT GIN RICKEY

Yield: 1 Drink
Active Time: 2 Minutes
Total Time: 2 Minutes

2 peeled cucumber ribbons

2 sprigs of fresh mint

2 oz. Empress 1908 Gin

½ oz. Simple Syrup (see page 243)

Pinch of kosher salt

1 oz. fresh lime juice

1 oz. club soda

1   Spiral the cucumber ribbons around the inside of a highball glass. Add the mint and ice.

2   Add the gin, simple syrup, salt, and lime juice and gently stir to combine.

3   Top with the club soda and enjoy.

SOUTHERN TAILGATE BOARD

Football is religion down South, and the pre- and post-game spreads are taken almost as seriously as the game, as you'll see when you taste this board of Southern classics.

Yield: 4 to 6 Servings

½ cup Pimento Cheese (see page 136)

2 oz. Pickled Red Onions (see page 139)

1 lb. Tasso Pork Tenderloin (see page 141), sliced

½ lb. Cornbread (see page 140)

1 Place the Pimento Cheese in a bowl and place it in the center of the board.

2 Divide the Pickled Red Onions between two small ramekins and place one to the left of the Pimento Cheese and the other to the right.

3 Arrange some of the pork in a line at the bottom of one ramekin.

4 Distribute the Cornbread around the board, fill in any gaps with the remaining pork, and enjoy.

PIMENTO CHEESE

Yield: 2 Cups
Active Time: 30 Minutes
Total Time: 40 Minutes

½ cup cream cheese, softened

3 oz. peppadew peppers, strained and finely diced

1 tablespoon finely chopped Garlic Confit (see page 241)

¼ cup mayonnaise

1 cup grated sharp cheddar cheese

1 tablespoon chopped fresh chives

1 tablespoon chopped fresh parsley

Salt and pepper, to taste

1   Place the cream cheese in a food processor and pulse for about 30 seconds.

2   Add the peppadew peppers, Garlic Confit, and mayonnaise and pulse for 1 to 2 minutes, until the mixture is thoroughly combined.

3   Add half of the cheddar cheese and pulse to incorporate.

4   Remove the mixture from the food processor and transfer it to a bowl. Add the remaining cheddar cheese, chives, and parsley and stir until thoroughly incorporated.

5   Season the pimento cheese with salt and pepper and serve.

PICKLED RED ONIONS

Yield: 2 Quarts

Active Time: 30 Minutes

Total Time: 2 Hours and 35 Minutes

1½ cups water

¾ cup rice vinegar

3 tablespoons kosher salt

½ cup plus 2 tablespoons sugar

3 large red onions, sliced thin

2 whole cloves

1 star anise pod, broken up

1　Place the water, vinegar, salt, and sugar in a small saucepan and bring to a gentle simmer, stirring to dissolve the salt and sugar.

2　Divide the onions, cloves, and star anise among two large mason jars.

3　Pour the brine into the jars and gently stir.

4　Place a lid on the jar, but do not fully tighten it. Chill the pickled red onions in the refrigerator overnight before serving.

Yield: 8 to 10 Servings

Active Time: 25 Minutes

Total Time: 1 Hour and 10 Minutes

1 cup all-purpose flour

1 cup cornmeal

1 tablespoon baking powder

1 teaspoon kosher salt

Pinch of cayenne pepper

1 egg

¾ cup sugar

¼ teaspoon pure vanilla extract

2 tablespoons unsalted butter, melted

2 tablespoons extra-virgin olive oil

¼ cup buttermilk

⅓ cup milk

1 tablespoon honey

CORNBREAD

1. Preheat the oven to 400°F. Coat a round 9-inch cake pan with nonstick cooking spray.

2. Place the flour, cornmeal, baking powder, salt, and cayenne in a mixing bowl and whisk to combine.

3. Crack the egg into a separate bowl and whisk in the sugar and vanilla. Slowly stream in the butter and olive oil, whisking until thoroughly combined.

4. Slowly stream in the buttermilk, milk, and honey, whisking until thoroughly combined.

5. Add the dry mixture and whisk until it comes together as a smooth batter.

6. Pour the batter into the greased pan, place it in the oven, and bake until the top is golden brown and a toothpick inserted into the center comes out clean, 35 to 40 minutes.

7. Remove the cornbread from the oven and let it cool slightly before serving.

TASSO PORK TENDERLOIN

Yield: 8 Servings
Active Time: 30 Minutes
Total Time: 28 Hours and 30 Minutes

2 (1 lb.) pork tenderloins, silverskin removed

½ cup to ¾ cup Standard Cure (see page 246)

½ teaspoon cayenne pepper

1 tablespoon granulated garlic

1 tablespoon granulated onion

1 tablespoon black pepper

1 tablespoon coriander

1 tablespoon paprika

1 teaspoon allspice

1 tablespoon dried oregano

1   Place the pork on a pan and rub it with the Standard Cure. Cover the pan with plastic wrap and chill it in the refrigerator for 24 hours.

2   Place the remaining ingredients in a bowl and whisk to combine.

3   Remove the pork from the refrigerator and rinse it under cold water. Pat the pork dry and sprinkle the seasoning mixture over it. Return the pork to the refrigerator.

4   Preheat a smoker to 200ºF.

5   Place the pork in the smoker and smoke it until the internal temperature is 155°F.

6   Remove the pork from the smoker and let it rest for 30 minutes.

7   Chill the pork in the refrigerator before slicing it thin and serving.

ENTERTAINING A LARGE GROUP BOARD

Yield: Ingredients for 1 Serving

½ oz. mustard

1½ oz. dips and spreads

½ oz. jams or fruit preserves (apricot jam)

2 oz. assorted bread (cornbread, baguette, rolls)

2 oz. crackers

1½ oz. assorted charcuterie (salami, pork pâté, prosciutto)

1 oz. assorted cheeses (cheddar, brie, goat, blue)

½ oz. dehydrated fruit (apples, apricots, cherries, cranberries)

½ oz. fresh fruit (grapes, figs)

1 oz. pickled vegetables

½ oz. assorted nuts

½ oz. wild-card ingredient (popcorn, pretzels)

From bold and delicate to savory and sweet, each element of this board is created to accommodate the myriad of preferences that inevitably exists in a big group. Whether it's a festive occasion, a large gathering of friends, or an outright event, this board promises to deliver. Simply multiply the ingredients provided by the number of people you're expecting, and you've got a can't miss crowd-pleaser.

1 Place any ingredients that need to be contained in a ramekin and arrange them on the board, making sure there is plenty of space between them.

2 Distribute the bread over the board.

3 Arrange the charcuterie and cheese on the board, fill in any gaps with the fruit, pickled vegetables, nuts, and wild-card ingredient, and enjoy.

HALLOWEEN BOARD

Embrace your spooky side with this Halloween-themed board—ghoulish décor is a must, of course, but consider also choosing a cheese with a black rind, as it will enhance the mysterious look of your spread.

Yield: 6 to 8 Servings

12 Chocolate Cake Truffles (see page 148)

4 oz. chocolate-covered almonds

4 oz. dried apricots

2 oz. dried cranberries

4 oz. salami

4 oz. prosciutto

4 oz. sharp cheddar cheese

4 oz. mild white cheddar cheese

3 oz. apple chips

4 oz. cured pork sausage

¼ cup whole-grain mustard

3 oz. crackers

1 Place your Halloween decorations on a board. We opted for a skeleton and pumpkins, but you can go with whatever you have! Just make sure the biggest decoration is in the middle of the board and any smaller ones are on the edges.

2 Mentally section the board into four parts. Arrange a combination of all of the ingredients in each section, playing around with the groupings of ingredients and how you lay them out, and enjoy.

CHOCOLATE CAKE

Yield: 1 Cake
Active Time: 30 Minutes
Total Time: 1 Hour and 10 Minutes

¾ cup boiling water

½ cup unsweetened cocoa powder

1¼ cups all-purpose flour

1 teaspoon baking powder

½ teaspoon baking soda

1 teaspoon kosher salt

1 egg

1 egg yolk

1 cup sugar

2 teaspoons pure vanilla extract

⅓ cup plus 1 tablespoon extra-virgin olive oil

¼ cup sour cream

1   Preheat the oven to 350°F and coat a round 9-inch cake pan with nonstick cooking spray.

2   Place the boiling water in a heatproof mixing bowl, add the cocoa powder, and whisk the mixture is smooth. Set the mixture aside.

3   Place the flour, baking powder, baking soda, and salt in a separate mixing bowl and whisk to combine. Set the mixture aside.

4   Place the egg, egg yolk, sugar, and vanilla in the work bowl of a stand mixer fitted with the whisk attachment and whip on medium speed until the mixture becomes light and airy, about 2 minutes.

5   Add the sour cream and olive oil and whip until they have been incorporated.

6   Set the mixer to low speed and slowly stream in the cocoa mixture until it has been incorporated.

7   Add the dry mixture and whip until it comes together as a smooth batter, scraping down the work bowl as needed.

8   Pour the batter into the cake pan, tap it on the counter a few times to remove any air bubbles, and place the cake in the oven. Bake until a toothpick inserted into the center of the cake comes out clean, 35 to 40 minutes.

9   Remove the cake from the oven and let it cool completely before using it to make the Chocolate Cake Truffles.

HALLOWEEN BOARD, SEE PAGE 144

CHOCOLATE CAKE TRUFFLES

Yield: 20 Truffles
Active Time: 30 Minutes
Total Time: 2 Hours

Chocolate Cake (see page 145), chopped

1 cup sweetened condensed milk

1 lb. dark chocolate morsels

1 Place the chocolate cake and condensed milk in the work bowl of a stand mixer fitted with the paddle attachment and beat until the mixture is smooth and there are no longer any large clumps, 20 to 30 seconds.

2 Line a baking sheet with parchment paper. Scoop out 1 oz. portions of the cake mixture, form them into balls, and place them on the baking sheet.

3 Place the truffles in the freezer until they have hardened, about 1 hour.

4 Fill a medium saucepan halfway with water and bring to a simmer. Place the chocolate morsels in a heatproof bowl and set it over the simmering water. Let the chocolate sit until it has melted, stirring occasionally. Remove the melted chocolate from heat.

5 Remove the truffles from the freezer and roll them in the melted chocolate until they are completely coated. Place them back on the baking sheet, place them in the refrigerator, and let the chocolate set before serving.

HARVEST BOARD

Modern commerce has made it possible to enjoy this board at any time of year, but we feel it should really only be an option during fig season, which tends to come at the beginning of fall, just as the weather starts to cool, but well before it starts to wear.

Yield: 2 to 4 Servings

8 Brûléed Fig & Goat Cheese Bites (see page 152)

4 oz. prosciutto or country ham

2 oz. toasted pecans

4 sprigs of fresh thyme, halved, for garnish

1 Arrange the Brûléed Fig & Goat Cheese Bites on a board.

2 Arrange the prosciutto on the board, laying some slices across the board and folding the others.

3 Fill in any gaps with the toasted pecans.

4 Garnish with the thyme and enjoy.

BRÛLÉED FIG & GOAT CHEESE BITES

Yield: 4 Servings
Active Time: 25 Minutes
Total Time: 25 Minutes

4 fresh figs

Salt, to taste

2 oz. fresh goat cheese

2 tablespoons crushed toasted pecans

Zest of 1 lemon

1 to 2 tablespoons sugar (to torch)

1. Halve the figs, cutting through the stems, and place them on a flame-proof tray or board.

2. Season the figs with salt and set them aside.

3. Place the goat cheese, toasted pecans, and lemon zest in a bowl and stir until thoroughly combined. Season the mixture with a few pinches of salt.

4. Top each piece of fig with about 1½ teaspoons of the goat cheese mixture.

5. Sprinkle the sugar on top of the goat cheese mixture and caramelize it using a kitchen torch, moving in a subtle, circular motion.

6. Let the figs cool slightly and the sugar harden before serving.

DREAMS OF ITALY BOARD

A trip to Sicily is closer than you think—all that's required is this board, which centers around a deconstructed Caprese salad, and a little imagination. We have found that the board looks the best when it has a natural feel, and looks like each ingredient is simply where it has fallen.

Yield: 6 to 8 Servings

4 oz. Tomato & Herb Focaccia (see page 161)

4 oz. burrata

4 oz. fresh mozzarella cheese

4 oz. assorted salumi (Italian cured meats)

1 lb. ripe tomatoes, pieces cut in various shapes and sizes

Salt and pepper, to taste

½ lb. Pork Meatballs (see page 158)

2 oz. Pesto (see page 155)

2 tablespoons balsamic vinegar

2 tablespoons extra-virgin olive oil

2 oz. fresh basil, for garnish

1 Cut the focaccia into pieces that are various shapes and sizes and distribute them over a board.

2 Scatter large dollops of the burrata and pieces of mozzarella over the board. Do the same with the salumi.

3 Season the tomatoes with salt and pepper and arrange them on the board, making sure you spread them out. Feel free to overlap the tomatoes with the other ingredients.

4 Fill in any gaps with the meatballs. Distribute the Pesto in spoonfuls, having some drop directly on the board and on the ingredients.

5 Drizzle the vinegar and olive oil over everything, garnish with the fresh basil, and enjoy.

Yield: 1½ Cups
Active Time: 30 Minutes
Total Time: 35 Minutes

1 cup fresh parsley

4 cups fresh basil

¼ cup fresh thyme

½ cup fresh mint

¾ cup grated Parmesan cheese

10 cloves of Garlic Confit (see page 241)

¾ cup extra-virgin olive oil

Zest of 2 lemons

Salt, to taste

PESTO

1 Separate the herbs and bring water to a boil in a medium pot. Prepare an ice bath.

2 Add half of the parsley and half of the basil to the boiling water and cook for about 30 seconds. Remove the herbs from the boiling water and shock them in the ice bath until they are cold. Squeeze the herbs to remove any excess water and set them aside.

3 Place the blanched basil and parsley in a food processor, add the remaining ingredients, including the remaining basil and parsley, and puree on low speed until everything is chopped and combined, but before it is a smooth puree.

4 Taste, adjust the seasoning as necessary, and chill the pesto in the refrigerator before serving.

DREAMS OF ITALY BOARD, SEE PAGE 154

PORK MEATBALLS

Yield: 20 Meatballs
Active Time: 40 Minutes
Total Time: 1 Hour

1 lb. ground pork

2 teaspoons sugar

2 teaspoons paprika

2 teaspoons dried oregano

2 teaspoons dried basil

1 tablespoon chopped
fresh Italian parsley

4 large garlic cloves,
chopped

2 tablespoons minced
yellow onion

1 teaspoon red pepper
flakes

¼ teaspoon black pepper

1 tablespoon kosher salt

1 tablespoon red wine
vinegar

2 egg yolks

1 teaspoon toasted fennel
seeds

½ teaspoon toasted
coriander seeds

1   Place the ground pork in a large bowl and add all of the remaining ingredients, except for the vinegar, egg yolks, fennel seeds, and coriander seeds. Work the mixture until it is thoroughly combined.

2   Add the vinegar and stir to incorporate. Incorporate the egg yolks 1 at a time, add the fennel and coriander seeds, and stir until they are evenly distributed.

3   Cook a small portion of the mixture in the microwave until it is cooked through. Taste and adjust the seasoning of the mixture as necessary.

4   Preheat the oven to 350°F and coat a baking sheet with nonstick cooking spray.

5   Form the mixture into 1 oz. balls and place them on the baking sheet.

6   Place the meatballs in the oven and cook until they have an internal temperature of 160°F, 12 to 15 minutes.

7   Remove the meatballs from the oven and let them cool slightly before serving.

TOMATO & HERB FOCACCIA

Yield: 1 Loaf
Active Time: 25 Minutes
Total Time: 3 Hours and 45 Minutes

5½ oz. lukewarm water (about 90°F)

2 teaspoons active dry yeast

10 oz. bread flour

2 teaspoons sugar

1 tablespoon kosher salt

2 tablespoons extra-virgin olive oil, plus more as needed

1 tablespoon chopped fresh sage

1 tablespoon chopped fresh basil

8 cherry tomatoes

Coarse sea salt, for topping

1   Place the water and yeast in a mixing bowl, gently stir, and let the mixture sit until it starts to foam, about 10 minutes.

2   Place the flour, sugar, salt, and olive oil in the work bowl of a stand mixer fitted with the dough hook and whisk to combine.

3   Add the yeast mixture to the work bowl and work the mixture on low speed until it comes together as a smooth dough, about 7 minutes.

4   Add the sage and basil and work the dough until they are easily distributed. The dough should be slightly tacky to the touch but should release from the sides and bottom of the bowl.

5   Coat a large bowl with olive oil and place the dough in it. Cover the bowl loosely with plastic wrap and let the dough rest in a naturally warm spot until it has doubled in size, about 1 hour.

6   Coat a round 9-inch cake pan with olive oil. Punch down the dough, place it in the pan, and stretch the dough to the edge of the pan.

7   Press down on the dough to make indents in it. Press the cherry tomatoes into the dough, making sure they are evenly distributed. Cover the pan with plastic wrap and let the dough rest in a naturally warm spot until it has doubled in size, about 2 hours.

8   Preheat the oven to 375°F. Drizzle olive oil over the focaccia and sprinkle coarse sea salt over the top.

9   Place the focaccia in the oven and bake until the top is a beautiful golden brown and it sounds hollow when you tap on it, 15 to 20 minutes. Remove the focaccia from the oven and let it cool completely before serving.

FARMERS MARKET BOARD

Yield: 6 to 8 Servings

½ cup dip

2 oz. red bell pepper, sliced

2 oz. carrots, sliced into batons

2 oz. yellow squash, sliced into batons

2 oz. celery, sliced into batons

2 oz. radishes, cut into wedges

2 oz. green beans, blanched and patted dry

Vegetable Terrine (see page 165)

Tomato Water Gelee (see page 166)

2 oz. cherry tomatoes, sliced

4 oz. crackers

Fresh herbs, for garnish

Edible flowers, for garnish

A great board for those days when you got a bit carried away at the farmers market, bought absolutely everything, and now need preparations that can utilize such a haul. Call up your vegetarian friends and invite them over to share in this considerable, and considerably refined, bounty.

1 Place the dip in a small bowl or ramekin and place it onto the center of a small board.

2 Arrange the red pepper, carrots, squash, celery, radishes, and green beans around the dip.

3 Place the board in the center of a larger board or tile. Arrange the Vegetable Terrine on one side of the larger board and the Tomato Water Gelee on the other side, along with the sliced cherry tomatoes and crackers.

4 Garnish with fresh herbs and edible flowers and enjoy.

Extra-virgin olive oil, as needed

1 small yellow squash

1 small zucchini

Salt and pepper, to taste

1 red bell pepper

1 yellow bell pepper

2 tablespoons sliced cherry tomatoes

1 tablespoon fresh thyme

1 teaspoon chopped fresh sage

2 tablespoons chopped fresh basil

½ cup fresh tomato puree

¼ oz. powdered gelatin

VEGETABLE TERRINE

Yield: 6 Servings
Active Time: 30 Minutes
Total Time: 5 Hours and 15 Minutes

1 Preheat the oven to 425°F and coat a baking sheet with olive oil.

2 Cut the summer squash and zucchini into ½-inch-thick slices. Season with salt and pepper and then place them on the baking sheet with the bell peppers. Drizzle olive oil over the vegetables and place them in the oven. Roast the vegetables until they are tender, 30 to 40 minutes, turning them as necessary.

3 Remove the vegetables from the oven, transfer the bell peppers to a bowl, and cover the bowl with plastic wrap. Let the peppers steam for 10 minutes. Transfer the zucchini and squash to a cutting board.

4 Dice the zucchini and squash and transfer them to a bowl. Toss in the sliced cherry tomatoes, season with a few pinches of salt, and add the thyme, sage, and basil. Stir to combine and set the mixture aside.

5 Place the tomato puree in a small saucepan and whisk in the gelatin so that there are no clumps. Let the puree sit for 5 minutes so that the gelatin blooms.

6 Remove the skins and seed pods from the peppers and dice them. Drizzle some olive oil over the peppers, add them to the vegetable-and-herb mixture, and toss to combine. Set the mixture aside.

7 Place the tomato puree over medium heat and cook until everything is smooth, stirring occasionally. Season with salt, turn off the heat, and allow the puree to cool at room temperature for 5 minutes.

8 While the puree is cooling, prepare a terrine mold or the vessel you plan on setting the terrine in, coating it with nonstick cooking spray and then lining it with plastic wrap. Make sure to extend the plastic wrap over the sides of the terrine so that it is easy to remove once it has set.

9 When the puree has cooled slightly, pour it into the bowl with the vegetables and gently stir to combine. Immediately pour the mixture into the prepared terrine mold and press down to remove any air pockets. Make sure that everything is submerged in the tomato puree.

10 Place the terrine in the refrigerator and let it chill until it is completely set, about 4 hours.

11 Gently lift the terrine out of the mold and transfer it to a cutting board. Cut the terrine into slices of your desired thickness and serve chilled or at room temperature.

TOMATO WATER GELEE

Yield: 6 Servings

Active Time: 1 Hour and 25 Minutes

Total Time: 24 Hours

1 lb. tomatoes, diced

1 teaspoon kosher salt

¼ oz. powdered gelatin

1. Place the tomatoes in a bowl, season with the salt, and toss to combine.

2. Line a strainer with cheesecloth and place it over a bowl.

3. Transfer the tomatoes to the strainer and place a piece of cheesecloth on top. Place a 1 to 2 lb. object on top of the tomatoes and let them drain overnight in the refrigerator.

4. Prepare the container in which you will be setting the gelee, coating it with nonstick cooking spray and then lining it with plastic wrap. Make sure to extend the plastic wrap over the sides of the terrine so that it is easy to remove once it has set.

5. After the tomatoes have been adequately pressed, you should be left with about ⅔ cup of tomato water. Taste the tomato water and season it as necessary.

6. Separate the tomato water into two equal portions and sprinkle the powdered gelatin into one portion while whisking. Whisk until the mixture becomes smooth and has no clumps. Allow the mixture to sit for about 3 minutes so that the gelatin blooms.

7. Transfer the tomato-and-gelatin mixture to a small saucepan and gently warm it over low heat until the gelatin has dissolved.

8. Remove the pan from heat and let the mixture cool for 5 minutes. Add the other portion of tomato water and whisk to combine. Pour the mixture in the prepared container and chill the gelee in the refrigerator until it has set, about 2 hours.

9. Gently lift the gelee out of the container, remove the plastic wrap, and transfer the gelee to a cutting board. Cut the gelee into slices of your desired thickness and serve chilled or at room temperature.

THANKSGIVING BOARD

Sure, everything revolves around the big meal on T-Day, but your guests still need some snacks to whet their appetite—and you need a spread that will keep them out of the kitchen while you put the finishing touches on the main event.

Yield: 6 to 8 Servings

Baked Brie (see page 173)

½ cup Cranberry Sauce (see page 170)

1 small baguette

4 oz. crackers

6 oz. prosciutto

6 oz. mortadella

6 oz. sharp cheddar cheese

Fresh sage, for garnish

Fresh rosemary, for garnish

Fresh thyme, for garnish

1   Place the Baked Brie in the center of a board.

2   Place the Cranberry Sauce in a ramekin and place it in the top portion of the board.

3   Place the baguette on the left side of the board. Cut a few slices from the baguette and leave the rest of it whole.

4   Place the crackers on the right side of the board.

5   Fill in the gaps with the charcuterie and cheddar and garnish with sage, rosemary, and thyme. Decorate the board with Thanksgiving-related items and enjoy.

CRANBERRY SAUCE

Yield: 4 Cups
Active Time: 20 Minutes
Total Time: 45 Minutes

1 lb. fresh or frozen cranberries

½ lb. dried cranberries

1 cup orange juice

Zest of 1 orange

Zest and juice of 1 lemon

2 cinnamon sticks

3 whole cloves

1 star anise pod

1 cup sugar

2 pinches of kosher salt

1   Place all of the ingredients in a medium saucepan and bring to a simmer over medium heat.

2   Reduce the heat so that the sauce comes to a gentle simmer and cook, stirring occasionally, until the whole cranberries start to pop and the liquid has reduced. Keep in mind that the sauce will thicken as it cools.

3   Remove the pan from heat and let the sauce cool completely before serving.

Yield: 4 to 6 Servings
Active Time: 25 Minutes
Total Time: 45 Minutes

¼ cup diced apple

1 tablespoon chopped fresh sage

¼ cup dried cranberries

⅓ cup chopped pecans

¼ cup honey

½ teaspoon cinnamon

2 tablespoons apple butter or applesauce

2 pinches of kosher salt

Zest and juice of 1 lemon

1 (½ lb.) wheel of brie cheese

BAKED BRIE

1 Preheat the oven to 350°F and line a baking sheet with parchment paper.

2 Place the apple, sage, dried cranberries, pecans, honey, cinnamon, apple butter, salt, lemon zest, and lemon juice in a bowl and stir until thoroughly combined, making sure the honey and apple butter are evenly distributed.

3 Remove the brie from the wrapper and place it on the baking sheet. Spread the topping over the brie, place it in the oven, and bake until it softens slightly, about 12 minutes.

4 Remove the brie from the oven and let it rest for 2 to 3 minutes before serving.

MUFFALETTA BOARD

A build-your-own sandwich platter is one of the best places to start a board, and designing a spread around the muffuletta, one of the world's truly great sandwiches, is sure to leave your guests raving about your exceptional abilities as a host.

Yield: 6 to 8 Servings

Tapenade (see page 176)

1 lb. Genoa salami, sliced

1 lb. mortadella, sliced

1 lb. prosciutto or capicola, sliced

1 lb. soppressata, sliced

1 lb. provolone cheese, sliced

½ cup Aioli (see page 177)

8 muffuletta-style rolls, for serving

1   Place the Tapenade in a bowl and place it in the top right corner of a board.

2   Starting at the top of the board, arrange the salami in a curved row. Do the same with the mortadella, overlapping it with the salami. Repeat with the prosciutto, soppressata, and provolone.

3   Place the Aioli in a ramekin and place it on the bottom left of the board.

4   Serve with muffuletta-style rolls and enjoy.

TAPENADE

Yield: 8 Servings
Active Time: 5 Minutes
Total Time: 5 Minutes

1 cup mixed olives, pitted

½ cup giardiniera, drained

2 tablespoons capers

2 tablespoons chopped fresh Italian parsley

1 tablespoon chopped fresh basil

1 teaspoon fresh thyme

Zest of 1 lemon

¼ cup red wine vinegar

¼ cup extra-virgin olive oil

1. Place the olives, giardiniera, and capers in a food processor and pulse until chopped, combined, and no large chunks remain.

2. Transfer the mixture to a bowl, add the remaining ingredients, and stir to combine. Taste, adjust the seasoning as necessary, and serve.

2 tablespoons minced
Garlic Confit (see page 241)

2 egg yolks

¼ teaspoon Dijon mustard

½ teaspoon kosher salt

1 teaspoon fresh lemon
juice

2 dashes of Tabasco

2 dashes of Worcestershire
sauce

Pinch of black pepper

½ cup extra-virgin olive oil

AIOLI

1   Place all of the ingredients, except for the olive oil, in a bowl and
    whisk to combine.

2   While whisking continually, add the olive oil in a slow stream until it
    has emulsified and the aioli is light and airy.

3   Taste, adjust the seasoning as necessary, and serve.

TIME TO SHINE BOARD

This board provides an opportunity for you to show off your culinary skills to friends and family, featuring two forms of that notorious hard to-master measuring stick, pâté. While the bar is high for this board, the good news is that you can take your time, as the only hands-on preparation can be made ahead of time.

Yield: 6 to 8 Servings

2 portions of Chicken Liver Pâté (see page 198)

3 oz. whole-grain mustard

3 oz. Dijon mustard

1 lb. Country Pork Pâté (see page 182), sliced

6 oz. saucisson, sliced

Cornichons, as desired

1 loaf of French bread, sliced and toasted

1   Place one portion of the Chicken Liver Pâté in the bottom left of a board and the other in the center.

2   Place the whole-grain mustard in a ramekin and place it near the top left of the board. Place the Dijon mustard in a ramekin and set it in the bottom right of the board.

3   Place the slices of Country Pork Pâté near the top of the board and the saucisson near the bottom of the board.

4   Fill in any gaps with cornichons and the slices of toasted bread and enjoy.

FRENCH COUNTRYSIDE BOARD

Capture the rustic charm of the French countryside with this board and pay tribute to the tasteful, thoughtful simplicity that defines the idyllic rural landscape of France. The rich pâté pairs nicely with the cornichons' tangy crunch, while the whole-grain mustard provides a zesty contrast.

Yield: 4 to 6 Servings

1 lb. Country Pork Pâté (see page 182), sliced

4 oz. cornichons

3 oz. Dijon mustard

½ loaf of French bread, sliced

1 Place the pâté on a board. You can either arrange the slices in a row or stack them on top of one another.

2 Place the cornichons in a ramekin and the mustard in another one. Place the ramekins on the board, on opposite sides of the pâté.

3 Distribute the slices of bread over the board and enjoy.

COUNTRY PORK PÂTÉ

Yield: 10 to 12 Servings
Active Time: 35 Minutes
Total Time: 8 Hours

1   Place the work bowl of a stand mixer in the freezer for 30 minutes. This is important because you do not want the pork fat to melt when you are making the pâté, because then it will have a grainy texture as opposed to smooth and silky.

2   Place the olive oil in a large skillet and warm it over medium heat. Add the onion, season with salt, and cook, stirring occasionally, until it is translucent, about 3 minutes.

3   Add the garlic, reduce the heat to low, and cook, stirring continually, for 2 minutes. Transfer the mixture to a bowl and let it cool.

4   Preheat the oven to 300°F and bring 4 cups of water to a boil. Prepare a terrine mold or the vessel you plan on setting the pâté in, coating it with nonstick cooking spray and then lining it with parchment paper. Make sure to extend the parchment paper over the sides of the mold so that the pâté is easy to remove once it has set.

5   Crack the eggs into a small bowl and whisk to scramble. Add the brandy and heavy cream and whisk to combine. Add the flour and whisk until the mixture is smooth.

6   Remove the stand mixer's work bowl from the freezer and add the ground pork, sage, thyme, curing salt, pepper, Pâté Spice, and onion mixture. Fit the stand mixer with the paddle attachment and beat the mixture on low speed until it is combined, about 30 seconds.

7   With the mixer running, slowly stream in the egg mixture until it is just combined.

8   Add the pistachios and dried cherries and beat until they have been evenly distributed.

9   Cook a small amount of the mixture in the microwave until cooked through. Taste and adjust the seasoning as necessary.

10 Pack the pâté mixture into the prepared mold and tap it on the counter to remove any air pockets. Cover the mold with aluminum foil, place it in a roasting pan, and fill the roasting pan with boiling water until it comes halfway up the sides of the mold.

11 Place the pâté in the oven and cook until the internal temperature is 160°F, about 1½ hours.

12 Remove the pâté from the oven and carefully remove the mold from the roasting pan. Let the pâté cool to room temperature and transfer it to the refrigerator. Place a 2 lb. weight on top of the pâté to press out any air pockets and chill it overnight.

13 Gently lift the pâté out of the mold and transfer it to a cutting board. Cut the pâté into slices of your desired thickness and serve chilled or at room temperature.

2 tablespoons extra-virgin olive oil

¼ cup diced yellow onion

Salt, to taste

1 tablespoon chopped garlic

3 whole eggs

3 tablespoons brandy

¾ cup heavy cream

1 oz. all-purpose flour

2 lbs. ground pork

2 tablespoons chopped fresh sage

2 tablespoons fresh thyme

⅛ teaspoon pink curing salt #1

1 teaspoon black pepper

1 teaspoon Pâté Spice (see page 247)

¼ cup shelled pistachios

¼ cup dried cherries

IT'S GOURD SEASON BOARD

The Roasted Gourd Hummus provides subtle sweetness to the board, and the Candied Pumpkin Seeds lend the necessary crunch. Wedges of Cranberry Goat Cheese create a fusion of sweet and tangy flavors, while the delicate slices of saucisson bring a savory element to this board, which promises to be as playful and comforting as the season itself.

Yield: 10 to 12 Servings

Roasted Gourd Hummus
(see page 186)

½ lb. Country Pork Pâté
(see page 182), sliced

½ lb. crackers

Cranberry Goat Cheese
(see page 213), cut into
wedges

6 oz. saucisson, sliced

2 oz. apple chips

3 oz. dried cranberries

3 oz. dried apricots

4 oz. Candied Pumpkin
Seeds (see page 189)

Fresh herbs, for garnish

Marigolds, for garnish

1   Divide the hummus among two bowls and place them on opposite sides of a board.

2   Place the slices of pâté alongside one bowl of hummus, following the shape of the bowl. Arrange the crackers next to the other bowl of hummus.

3   Place the wedges of Cranberry Goat Cheese and slices of saucisson near the center of the board.

4   Fill in any gaps with apple chips, cranberries, apricots, Candied Pumpkin Seeds, and fall-related decorations, garnish with fresh herbs and marigolds, and enjoy.

ROASTED GOURD HUMMUS

Yield: 2 Cups
Active Time: 25 Minutes
Total Time: 1 Hour and 35 Minutes

¼ cup extra-virgin olive oil, plus more as needed

1 large squash or pumpkin, halved

1 tablespoon kosher salt

1 teaspoon cinnamon

1 teaspoon coriander

¼ teaspoon ground ginger

¼ teaspoon freshly grated nutmeg

Zest and juice of 1 lemon

2 tablespoons maple syrup

1 Preheat the oven to 350°F and coat a baking sheet with olive oil. Place the gourd, cut side down, on the baking sheet.

2 Place it in the oven and roast until the flesh is tender.

3 Remove the roasted gourd from the oven and let it cool slightly.

4 Scoop the seeds out of the roasted flesh and set them aside. Scoop the flesh into a bowl and then transfer 2 cups of it into a food processor.

5 Add all of the remaining ingredients, except for the olive oil, and blitz until smooth.

6 With the food processor running, stream in the olive oil until it has been incorporated.

7 Taste the hummus, adjust the seasoning as necessary, and serve.

CANDIED PUMPKIN SEEDS

Yield: 12 Servings
Active Time: 20 Minutes
Total Time: 1 Hour and 50 Minutes

3 egg whites

½ teaspoon pure vanilla extract

½ teaspoon cinnamon

1 teaspoon pumpkin spice

⅓ cup sugar

¾ lb. pumpkin seeds

1 teaspoon kosher salt

1   Preheat the oven to 225°F. Line a baking sheet with a Silpat mat and coat it with nonstick cooking spray.

2   Place the egg whites in the work bowl of a stand mixer fitted with the whisk attachment. Make sure that the bowl is very clean and that none of the egg yolks got in with the egg whites, as grease and fats from the egg yolk make the whites more difficult to whip.

3   Add the vanilla, cinnamon, and pumpkin spice to the egg whites and begin whipping the mixture at low speed for 10 seconds. Raise the speed to medium-high and whip until the egg whites become frothy and start to increase in volume. Slowly stream in the sugar and whip until the egg whites hold soft peaks and are smooth and glossy. Remove the work bowl from the stand mixer and gently add the pumpkin seeds to the whipped egg whites. Fold to combine.

4   Spread the pumpkin seeds on the baking sheet in an even layer and season them with salt. Place the pumpkin seeds in the oven and bake for 30 minutes.

5   Remove the pumpkin seeds from the oven and use a rubber spatula to lift them from the sheet and break them up. Once all of the large clumps are broken up, spread the pumpkin seeds on the sheet in an even layer, return them from the oven, and bake for another 30 minutes.

6   Remove the pumpkin seeds from the oven and use a rubber spatula to lift them from the sheet and break them up. Once all of the large clumps are broken up, spread the pumpkin seeds on the sheet in an even layer, return them from the oven, and bake until they are completely dry, about 30 minutes.Remove the pumpkin seeds from the oven and let them cool completely before serving or storing in an airtight container.

SPANISH TAPAS BOARD

This board features the best of those traditional Spanish snacks that have become a global phenomenon, tapas. The sweetness of the figs pairs wonderfully with the salty richness of the prosciutto, and the Stuffed Dates are savory and nutty, creating a harmonious balance of flavors.

Yield: 2 to 4 Servings

4 oz. olives

4 oz. Manchego cheese

4 oz. aged Cabra cheese

4 oz. Spanish chorizo, sliced

4 prosciutto-wrapped figs

4 Stuffed Dates (see page 193)

4 oz. bread or crackers

1 Place the olives in a ramekin and place it on a board. Arrange the slices of cheese on the board and then place the chorizo in a corner of the board.

2 Fill in any gaps with the prosciutto-wrapped figs and Stuffed Dates and enjoy.

STUFFED DATES

Yield: 8 Dates
Active Time: 25 Minutes
Total Time: 25 Minutes

¼ cup mascarpone cheese

⅛ teaspoon cinnamon

⅛ teaspoon freshly grated nutmeg

Zest and juice of 1 lemon, plus more zest for garnish

⅛ teaspoon pure vanilla extract

Pinch of kosher salt

8 large dates, pitted

1   Place the mascarpone in a bowl, add the remaining ingredients, except for the dates, and stir until the mixture is thoroughly combined and light and airy.

2   Taste, adjust the seasoning as necessary, and then transfer the filling into a piping bag with no tip.

3   Gently cut each date lengthwise on one side so that the interior of the date is exposed, but the dates are not cut all the way through. Pipe the dates full of the filling and press each date from the sides so that the filling pokes out of the cut side.

4   Garnish with additional lemon zest and serve chilled or at room temperature.

WINTER

There are times when the bitter winds and rapidly disappearing daylight begin to wear a person down. It can seem like there's little to look forward to, which puts everyone on edge. Winter is a season where the need for warmth, comfort, and fun is at its highest. When the need for all those things arises, the best antidote is putting together a board for friends and family to gather around.

These spreads are certain to bring everyone together, wash away the blues everyone's built up over the seemingly endless stretch of bleak days, and set their sights on the good the world contains.

ELEVATED IN A PINCH BOARD

The holidays are when friends and family start to drop by unexpectedly, and they are also the time when you have the least bandwith to deal with such surprises. Luckily, this effortlessly impressive board ensures that everything is on point, no matter how harried you're feeling.

Yield: 2 Servings

½ cup Chicken Liver Pâté (see page 198)

1 loaf of French bread, sliced and toasted

1   About 30 minutes before you are going to be serving this board, remove the pâté from the refrigerator and scrape off any portion from the top that has oxidized and become gray. Let the pâté sit at room temperature for 30 minutes so that it warms slightly and becomes spreadable.

2   Arrange the pâté and toasted slices of French bread on a board and enjoy.

CHICKEN LIVER PÂTÉ

Yield: 4 Cups
Active Time: 25 Minutes
Total Time: 24 Hours

1 lb. fresh chicken livers

1 cup whole milk

1 tablespoon extra-virgin olive oil

½ cup diced yellow onion

¼ teaspoon freshly grated nutmeg

½ cup brandy

½ cup heavy cream

1 tablespoon kosher salt, plus more to taste

⅛ teaspoon pink curing salt #1

1½ teaspoons sugar

½ teaspoon black pepper

1 cup unsalted butter, diced

1 Place the chicken livers in a container and cover them with the whole milk. Chill them in the refrigerator overnight. This will help remove some of the blood and impurities from the livers.

2 Strain the chicken livers and rinse them under cold water.

3 Transfer the livers to a blender and set them aside.

4 Place eight 4 oz. ramekins on a sheet tray and preheat the oven to 250°F.

5 Warm a medium saucepan over medium-high heat. Add the olive oil, warm it, and then add the onion. Reduce the heat to medium-low and cook, stirring occasionally, until it is translucent, about 4 minutes.

6 Add the nutmeg and cook, stirring continually, for 30 seconds.

7 Remove the pan from heat and deglaze the pan with the brandy, scraping up any browned bits from the bottom. Place the pan over medium heat and cook until the brandy has reduced by half.

8 Add the heavy cream and cook until it has reduced by half, stirring to make sure it does not boil over.

9 While the heavy cream is reducing, add the salts, sugar, and black pepper to the livers in the blender and puree on high until smooth.

10 Remove the pan from heat and add about one-quarter of the butter to the cream. Stir until it has emulsified. Repeat with the remaining butter.

11 Transfer the cream-and-butter emulsion to the blender and puree on medium until everything is thorough combined. Strain the mixture through a fine-mesh sieve and season it with salt.

12 Divide the pâté among the ramekins, place them in the oven, and bake until they are set and no longer jiggle when shaken, about 8 minutes. Turn off the oven and let them rest for 10 minutes.

13 Remove the pâté from the oven, place it in the refrigerator, and let it chill completely before serving. Cover the pâté once it is cool if you are making it ahead of time.

NEED A VACATION BOARD

This board is not only tasty, it looks like a scene you'd encounter snorkeling in the tropics. Break out this one when the winter weather really starts to wear on you.

Yield: 6 to 8 Servings

12 oz. Pickled Shrimp (see page 202)

15 to 20 shrimp chips

4 oz. seaweed salad

10 seaweed crackers

15 sprigs of fresh dill

6 oz. gravlax or smoked salmon

1   Fill a bowl (preferably a clear glass bowl) with the Pickled Shrimp and place it in the center of the board.

2   Arrange the rest of the ingredients around the bowl so that they loosely resemble a seascape. Think of the shrimp chips as coral, the seaweed as itself, the dill as seagrass, and the salmon as a more colorful kind of coral.

NEED A VACATION BOARD, SEE PAGE 199

PICKLED SHRIMP

Yield: 4 Servings

Active Time: 20 Minutes

Total Time: 2 Hours and 30 Minutes

¾ lb. shrimp, shelled and deveined

½ cup rice vinegar

1 cup water

2 tablespoons kosher salt

¼ cup sugar

2 tablespoons pickling spice

2 tablespoons Old Bay Seasoning

Zest of 1 lemon

1   Place the shrimp in an even layer in a small, square baking dish. Place all of the remaining ingredients in a medium saucepan and bring it to a simmer, stirring to dissolve the salt and sugar.

2   Pour the brine over the shrimp, making sure that they are completely covered. Let the shrimp sit until they turn pink and are cooked through, about 5 minutes.

3   Place the baking dish in the refrigerator and chill the shrimp before serving.

LET'S CELEBRATE COUPES

A chic and innovative way to present a classic charcuterie spread, and one that will go perfect with a celebratory bottle of bubbly. Keep in mind that the ingredients are for 1 person, so you will need to do a little math to make sure everyone at the party is covered.

Yield: Ingredients for 1 Coupe

1 to 2 oz. cheese

1 to 2 oz. cured meat

4 crackers

1 oz. dried fruit

1 oz. pickles

Fresh herbs, for garnish

1 Place the cheese in a coupe. We recommend having a mix of cheeses of various sizes to supply different textures and flavors.

2 Fold or twist the cured meat and add it to the coupe.

3 Fill in any gaps with the crackers, dried fruit, and pickles.

4 Garnish with fresh herbs and enjoy.

VALENTINE'S DAY BOUQUET BOARD

A romantic and whimsical take on the traditional charcuterie board that is sure to create a romantic and indulgent atmosphere. When making this bouquet, focus on cutting everything into bite-size portions so that the charcuterie skewers can be easily enjoyed.

Yield: 2 to 4 Servings

3 oz. salami

4 oz. cured sausages, sliced

3 oz. cheese cubes

4 oz. fresh strawberries

2 oz. dried apricots

3 oz. prosciutto

2 oz. dried fruit mix (raisins, dried cranberries, and dried cherries)

3 oz. candied orange slices

1 oz. fresh mint

6 large sprigs of fresh lavender

1 oz. edible flowers (marigolds, oregano blossoms, nasturtium, etc.)

1   Fold a piece of brown craft paper into a rectangle, then fold the sides at an angle, creating a triangle. The bottom should be closed but the top should remain open. Tie a ribbon or a piece of twine around the middle or bottom of the triangle to secure it. Add flowers and herbs as decor.

2   Divide the salami, sausages, and cheese among 10 to 12 skewers, making sure to add strawberries and/or dried apricots to some of the skewers. The skewers should vary and not all be the same.

3   Place the skewers in the opening of the craft paper cone, placing them at different heights.

4   Twist the prosciutto and fill in any gaps. Repeat this process with any remaining charcuterie and the dried fruit.

5   Decorate the "bouquet" with the mint, lavender, candied orange slices, and edible flowers.

Yield: 6 to 8 Servings

1 oz. kale

4 oz. cooked turkey breast, sliced

3 oz. salami, sliced

3 oz. provolone cheese, sliced

4 oz. Rosemary Goat Cheese (see page 210), sliced

4 oz. Cranberry Goat Cheese (see page 213), sliced

2 oz. Pimento Cheese (see page 136)

2 oz. chili-lime cashews

1 oz. dried cranberries

1 oz. golden raisins

3 sprigs of fresh rosemary, cut into 2-inch pieces

Fresh herbs, for garnish

Edible flower blossoms, for garnish

Candied blood orange slices, for garnish

IT'S THE HOLIDAY SEASON WREATH

A wreath is a captivating way to present a spread of charcuterie, cheeses, and accompaniments while also evoking the festive spirit of the holiday season! This is the ideal centerpiece for your holiday party.

1 Place a 5-inch-wide bowl in the center of a large board or marble slab. Sprinkle half of the kale around the bowl to form a loose circle.

2 Scatter the turkey, salami, and cheeses on top and alongside the kale, following the circular shape.

3 Fill in gaps with the cashews, cranberries, raisins, and rosemary.

4 Garnish with fresh herbs, flower blossoms, and candied blood oranges and enjoy.

ROSEMARY GOAT CHEESE

Yield: 2 Servings
Active Time: 5 Minutes
Total Time: 5 Minutes

2 tablespoons chopped fresh rosemary

1 (4 oz.) log of goat cheese

1   Place the rosemary on a plate and roll the goat cheese over it, applying gentle pressure so that the rosemary sticks to every side of the log.

2   To serve, slice into small medallions.

CRANBERRY GOAT CHEESE

Yield: 2 Servings
Active Time: 5 Minutes
Total Time: 5 Minutes

2 tablespoons finely chopped dried cranberries

¼ teaspoon cinnamon

1 teaspoon balsamic vinegar

1 (4 oz.) log of goat cheese

1   Place the cranberries, cinnamon, and balsamic vinegar in a bowl and stir to combine. Spread the mixture over a plate or board.

2   Roll the goat cheese over the cranberry mixture, applying gentle pressure so that the mixture coats the log completely.

3   Chill the goat cheese in the refrigerator for 10 minutes.

4   To serve, slice the cheese into small medallions.

CRAFT NIGHT BOARD

T he winter is all about finding ways to pass the time and remain warm, and this board, which you can easily personalize to celebrate every single one of your crafting buddies, is a great way to ensure that craft night becomes a regular respite from the harsh outdoors.

Yield: 2 to 4 Servings

2 oz. crackers

2 oz. cheese, sliced or cubed

2 oz. salami

1 oz. dried fruit

2 oz. fresh fruit

1 oz. assorted nuts

4 candied orange slices

Fresh mint, for garnish

Edible flowers, for garnish

1 Cut along the edges of a papier mâché number with an X-ACTO knife. Pull off the top of the cut side and remove any cardboard filler, making sure the number is hollow inside.

2 Clean the edges, tearing off the little stray bits. Fill the inside of the number with either tissue paper or parchment paper.

3 Arrange the crackers, cheese, and salami on top of the paper.

4 Fill in any gaps with the fruit, nuts, and candied orange slices. Garnish with mint and edible flowers and enjoy.

CHRISTMAS TIME IS HERE BOARD

A board that captures the magic of the holiday season, curating rich cheeses, the elegance of the holiday-themed brie, the savory allure of cured meats, and the sweetness of jams.

Yield: 2 to 4 Servings

Christmas Brie (see page 218)

1 oz. golden raisins

Fresh rosemary, as needed

4 oz. salami

4 oz. prosciutto

4 oz. cheddar cheese, cubed in a block

4 oz. goat cheese, cut into wedges

Fresh sage, for garnish

Crackers or bread, for serving

1 Place the Christmas Brie at the top of the board and surround it with golden raisins and rosemary, creating something of a Christmas wreath.

2 Fold the salami in quarters and place it on an empty side of the board, accordion-like. Distribute the prosciutto over the board.

3 Arrange the cheeses on the board, garnish with fresh sage, and enjoy with crackers or bread.

CHRISTMAS BRIE

Yield: 6 Servings
Active Time: 20 Minutes
Total Time: 20 Minutes

1 (½ lb.) wheel of brie cheese

1 to 2 oz. jam, butter, or preserves

1   Turn your brie on its side so that it is standing upright.

2   Slice the brie in half at its equator and place each piece flat on a cutting board.

3   Use a Christmas-themed cookie cutter to cut a shape into the center of one of the pieces.

4   Place the cut-out piece of brie on top of the other half and fill that hole with the jam, butter, or preserves. Serve immediately.

SUPER BOWL BOARD

The big game needs an equally outsized board, and this full-freighted offering is sure to fit the bill.

Yield: 4 Servings

Stromboli (see page 224)

¼ cup Blue Cheese Ranch (see page 226)

¼ cup Homemade Hot Sauce (see page 223)

Confit Chicken Wings (see page 222)

12 slices of prosciutto, salami, or pepperoni-wrapped mozzarella sticks

4 oz. celery sticks

4 oz. carrot chips

1 Cut a couple of slices from the Stromboli and set them aside. Place the rest of the Stromboli in the center of a board and then distribute the remaining slices over the board.

2 Place the Blue Cheese Ranch in a ramekin and place it next to the Stromboli.

3 Place the hot sauce in a ramekin and place it and the chicken wings on the opposite side from the Blue Cheese Ranch.

4 Fill in any gaps with the prosciutto, celery, and carrots and enjoy.

CONFIT CHICKEN WINGS

Yield: 12 Wings
Active Time: 20 Minutes
Total Time: 20 Hours and 30 Minutes

12 chicken wings

4 cups Basic Brine (see page 244)

2 cups rendered chicken, pork, or duck fat, plus more as needed

1   Place the chicken wings in the brine and refrigerate for 16 hours.

2   Remove the wings from the brine, rinse them under cold water, and pat them dry.

3   Preheat the oven to 275°F. Place the wings in a Dutch oven, pour the rendered fat over them, and cover the pot. Bake the wings in the oven until they are tender but do not fall apart, about 2 hours.

4   Remove the wings from the oven, remove them from the fat, and let them cool completely before frying.

5   Add rendered fat to a large, deep cast-iron skillet until it is about 1 inch deep and warm it to 350°F. You do not want to use the fat that you cooked the wings in because it may have some liquid from the wings trapped inside it that can spatter when heated to high temperatures.

6   Working in batches of 2 or 3, gently slip the wings into the hot oil and fry until they are crispy and golden brown, about 5 minutes.

7   Remove the wings from the hot oil and place them on a paper towel–lined plate to drain and cool slightly before serving.

1 tablespoon extra-virgin olive oil

1 cup diced yellow onion

Salt, to taste

5 oz. jalapeño chile peppers, stems and seeds removed, chopped

3 oz. Fresno chile peppers, stems and seeds removed, chopped

2 tablespoons chopped garlic

4 oz. Peppadew Peppers, chopped

1 cup Peppadew Pepper brine

½ cup apple cider vinegar

¾ cup water

HOMEMADE HOT SAUCE

1   Warm a medium saucepan over medium-high heat. Add the olive oil, warm it, and add the onion. Season with salt, reduce the heat to medium-low, and cook, stirring occasionally, until the onion is translucent, about 3 minutes.

2   Add the chile peppers, season with salt, and cook, stirring occasionally, for 2 minutes.

3   Add the garlic and cook, stirring continually, for 1 minute.

4   Add the Peppadew Peppers, brine, vinegar, and water, raise the heat to medium-high, and bring to a boil.

5   Reduce the heat so that the mixture simmers and cook for 30 minutes.

6   Transfer the mixture to a blender and puree until it is smooth. Taste, adjust the seasoning as necessary, and serve. If the sauce is too spicy, add ¼ cup of olive oil or butter, or honey to taste and puree it until it has been incorporated.

STROMBOLI

Yield: 8 Servings
Active Time: 25 Minutes
Total Time: 50 Minutes

2 tablespoons extra-virgin olive oil, plus more as needed

1 Pillsbury Pizza Crust

½ cup marinara sauce

12 thin slices of provolone cheese

10 thin slices of pepperoni

¼ cup grated Parmesan cheese

1   Preheat the oven to 400°F and coat a baking sheet with olive oil.

2   Roll the pizza crust into a thin rectangle and spread the sauce over the dough, leaving a ½ inch border at each of the long ends.

3   Arrange the provolone in two rows in the center of the crust, overlapping the slices slightly. Repeat with the pepperoni, placing them on top of the provolone.

4   Sprinkle the Parmesan over the pepperoni and roll up the dough into a log, starting at the short end closest to you.

5   Place the stromboli on the baking sheet and brush the outside with the olive oil.

6   Place in the oven and bake until the dough is a deep golden brown on the outside, about 25 minutes.

7   Remove the stromboli from the oven and let it cool slightly before slicing and serving.

BLUE CHEESE RANCH

Yield: 1½ Cups
Active Time: 25 Minutes
Total Time: 25 Minutes

½ cup mayonnaise

1 tablespoon sour cream

1 tablespoon chopped fresh parsley

2 tablespoons chopped fresh chives

1 teaspoon chopped fresh dill

2 garlic cloves, minced

4 oz. blue cheese, broken into small chunks

2 tablespoons buttermilk

2 dashes of Tabasco

2 dashes of Worcestershire sauce

2 pinches of black pepper

¼ teaspoon kosher salt

1 Place all of the ingredients, except for half of the blue cheese, in a bowl and stir until the blue cheese has broken down and the ingredients are thoroughly combined.

2 Add the remaining blue cheese and gently stir to incorporate, making sure to retain some texture. Taste, adjust the seasoning as necessary, and serve.

ST. PATRICK'S DAY BOARD

At the heart of this board are tender slices of Corned Beef, a dish that embodies the essence of Irish comfort food. The Potato Croquettes add a touch of heartiness, the Pickled Cabbage supplies a tantalizing crunch, and Irish cheddar balances everything out.

Yield: 6 to 8 Servings

2 lbs. Corned Beef (see page 229)

6 oz. Pickled Cabbage (see page 85)

Potato Croquettes (see page 231)

6 oz. Irish cheddar cheese, cut into cubes and wedges

Nasturtiums, for garnish

1 Slice some of the Corned Beef and leave some unsliced. Place it on the right side of a board.

2 Place the Pickled Cabbage in a ramekin and place it beside the Corned Beef, close to the bottom of the board.

3 Place the croquettes in a bowl or basket and place them to the left of the Corned Beef.

4 Fill in any gaps with the wedges and cubes of Irish cheddar.

5 Garnish with nasturtiums and enjoy.

Yield: 10 Servings

Active Time: 45 Minutes

Total Time: 4 Days and 8 Hours

CORNED BEEF

FOR THE BRINE

8 cups water

¾ cup kosher salt

¼ cup sugar

2 teaspoons pink curing salt #1

3 garlic cloves, smashed

1 bunch of fresh thyme

1 tablespoon Pickling Spice (see page 245)

FOR THE CORNED BEEF

2½ lbs. beef brisket

1 tablespoon Pickling Spice

4 cups chicken or beef stock

4 cups water

1 tablespoon kosher salt

1   To prepare the brine, place all of the ingredients in a large pot and bring it to a gentle simmer, stirring to dissolve the salt and sugar. Remove the pot from heat and let it cool completely.

2   To begin preparations for the corned beef, place the brisket in the cooled brine and weigh it down with something to ensure that it stays submerged. Brine the brisket in the refrigerator for 4 days.

3   Remove the brisket from the brine and rinse it under cold water. Place the brisket in a pot, add the remaining ingredients for the corned beef, and bring to a gentle simmer.

4   Cover the pot and cook the brisket until it is very tender and the interior is about 180°F, about 4 hours.

5   Let the brisket rest in the broth for 40 minutes before slicing and serving. If you plan on serving the corned beef chilled, slice the brisket thinner than if you are serving it warm.

POTATO CROQUETTES

Yield: 14 Croquettes
Active Time: 25 Minutes
Total Time: 2 Hours and 15 Minutes

½ lb. Yukon Gold potatoes, peeled and diced

Salt, to taste

4 tablespoons unsalted butter, chilled and diced

1 teaspoon sour cream

¼ cup grated sharp cheddar cheese

1 egg yolk

1 tablespoon chopped fresh chives

Canola oil, as needed

½ cup all-purpose flour

2 whole eggs

¼ cup milk

1 cup fine bread crumbs

1 Place the potatoes in a large pot and cover them by 2 inches with cold water. Add a few pinches of salt and bring to a boil. Reduce the heat so that the potatoes simmer steadily and cook until the potatoes are tender, about 20 minutes.

2 Drain the potatoes and place them in the work bowl of a stand mixer fitted with the paddle attachment. Add the butter, sour cream, and cheddar and beat on a low speed until combined.

3 Add the egg yolk and chives and beat until they are incorporated. Taste and season with salt.

4 Line a baking sheet with parchment paper. Form 1 oz. portions of the mixture into balls and place them on the baking sheet. Place the baking sheet in the freezer and let the croquettes set for 30 minutes.

5 Add canola oil to a Dutch oven until it is about 2 inches deep and warm it to 350ºF.

6 Place the flour in a shallow bowl. Place the eggs in a separate shallow bowl, add the milk, and whisk to combine. Place the bread crumbs in a separate shallow bowl. Dredge the croquettes in the flour, egg wash, and bread crumbs until they are completely coated. Place the breaded croquettes back on the baking sheet.

7 Working in batches, gently slip the croquettes into the hot oil and fry until they are golden brown, 5 to 6 minutes.

8 Transfer the fried croquettes to a paper towel–lined plate to drain before serving.

MOVIE NIGHT BOARD

A perfect platter to enjoy on those nights when all you want to do is curl up on the couch and watch a movie with family or friends.

Yield: 2 to 4 Servings

6 oz. Bacon & Sage Caramel Corn (see page 235)

4 oz. cheese

4 oz. charcuterie

2 oz. cornichons or pickled vegetables

Bread or crackers, for serving

1   Place the Bacon & Sage Caramel Corn in a bowl and place the bowl in the center of a board or platter.

2   Arrange the cheese, charcuterie, and cornichons around the bowl of popcorn, serve with bread or crackers, and enjoy.

BACON & SAGE CARAMEL CORN

Yield: 8 Cups
Active Time: 30 Minutes
Total Time: 1 Hour and 20 Minutes

8 cups popped popcorn

1 cup chopped bacon

½ cup brown sugar

¼ cup corn syrup

4 tablespoons unsalted butter

1 teaspoon kosher salt

¼ teaspoon baking soda

1 teaspoon pure vanilla extract

1 tablespoon chopped fresh sage

1   Preheat the oven to 250°F and coat a baking sheet with nonstick cooking spray. Fill the pan with the popcorn and set it aside.

2   Place the bacon in a Dutch oven and cook it over medium heat, stirring frequently, until the fat has rendered and the bacon is crispy, 6 to 8 minutes. Remove the bacon with a slotted spoon and place it on a paper towel–lined plate to drain.

3   Place the popcorn into the oven to warm it.

4   Place the brown sugar, corn syrup, butter, and salt in the bacon fat in the Dutch and bring the mixture to a boil, stirring continuously until the mixture reaches a boil.

5   Reduce the heat so that the caramel simmers. Cook for 5 minutes.

6   Remove the pot from the heat and stir in the baking soda, vanilla, sage, and bacon.

7   Remove the popcorn from the oven, pour the caramel over it, and stir until it is evenly coated.

8   Return the popcorn to the oven and bake for 45 minutes, stirring every 15 minutes or so.

9   Coat a large sheet of aluminum foil with nonstick cooking spray. Remove the caramel popcorn from the oven and spoon it onto the foil. Let it cool completely.

10 Break the popcorn apart and serve or store it in an airtight container.

LABELED CHARCUTERIE BOARD

Yield: 4 to 6 Servings

4 oz. pickles

5 oz. saucisson, sliced

4 oz. peach preserves

4 oz. brie cheese

6 oz. Country Pork Pâté
(see page 182), sliced

4 oz. Country Mustard (see
page 121)

4 oz. sharp cheddar cheese

4 oz. blue cheese

4 oz. goat cheese

6 oz. Vegetable Terrine (see
page 165)

¼ cup honey

6 oz. Smoked Salmon (see
page 55)

1 small baguette, sliced

Eating great food provides a tremendous opportunity to educate, as everyone's ears are a little more open during those times when they are being plied with delicious bite after delicious bite. Let everyone know exactly what they're eating, and make sure you do your research ahead of time, as the labels are sure to spark conversation and questions.

1   Lay out a large sheet of butcher paper and determine where you'd like to place your ingredients. Using a sharpie or a pen, write the name of each ingredient beside where it will be placed.

2   Place the ingredients on the butcher paper, ensuring that their associated labels can be read, and enjoy.

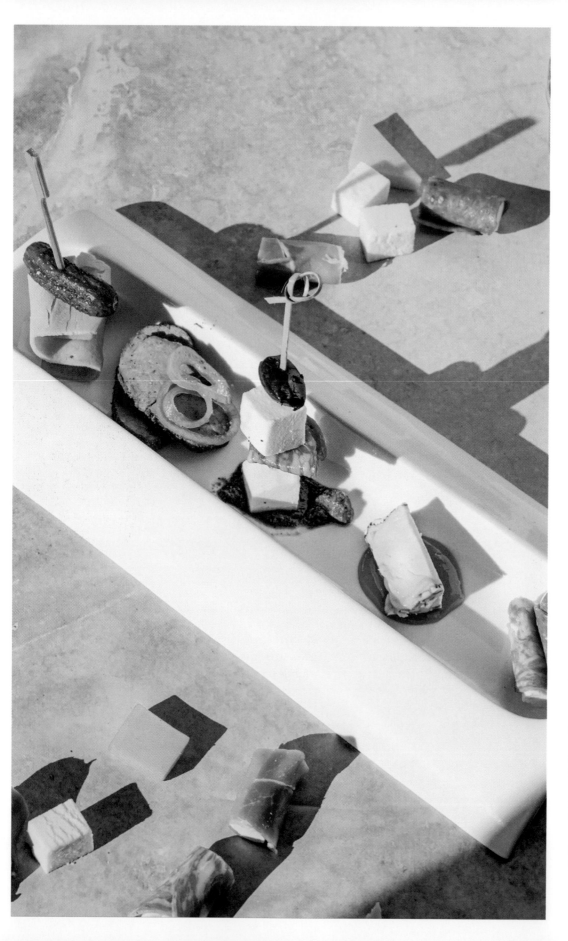

FOR THE SALUMI & MOZZARELLA BITE

3 pieces of mozzarella cheese

1 piece of pepperoni

1 piece of prosciutto

1 piece of Genoa salami

FOR THE HAM & CHEESE SKEWER

2 cubes of aged cheddar cheese

1 slice of black forest ham, cut into long ribbons

1 cornichon

FOR THE GOAT CHEESE & PEACH BITE

¼ teaspoon peach jam

1 small wedge of bloomy rind goat cheese

FOR THE OLIVE & SALAMI SKEWER

2 cubes of feta cheese

2 pitted kalamata olives

2 slices of Genoa salami, folded

¼ teaspoon Pesto (see page 155)

FOR THE PICKLED RED ONION & PORK BITE

2 slices of Tasso Pork Tenderloin (see page 141)

2 slices of Pickled Red Onion (see page 139)

PASSED HORS D'OEUVRES PLATTER

Yield: Ingredients for Single Servings

This board is the culmination of all you have learned, combining charcuterie, cheese, and other preparations into a series of small bites that are intended to be passed at a cocktail party or large event. The ingredients provided are meant to make a single appetizer, so make sure to multiply them by the number of guests.

1   To prepare the salumi & mozzarella bite, wrap each of the pieces of mozzarella with one of the cured meats. Cut them in half, thread them on skewers, and place them on the platter you plan on passing hors d'oeurves with.

2   To prepare the ham & cheese skewer, wrap a cube of cheddar with a ribbon of ham so that the ham only covers three sides of the cheese.

3   Place the second cube of cheese on top of the first one, making sure the ham is in between the two cubes. Fold the ham over the top block of cheese so that it is also wrapped around three sides of this cube.

4   Thread the cornichon onto a skewer, sliding the cornichon all the way to the top of the skewer.

5   Thread the ham-and-cheese onto the skewer so that it sits directly below the cornichon. Transfer the skewer to the platter.

6   To prepare the goat cheese & peach bite, place the jam directly on the platter and place the wedge of goat cheese directly on top of the jam.

7   To prepare the olive & salami skewer, thread a cube of feta and an olive onto a skewer. Fold the salami into triangles and thread them onto the skewer, making sure they are in the center. Push the salami up to meet the feta so that the salami is in the center of the skewer.

8   Add the remaining olive to the skewer, followed by the remaining cube of feta. Arrange the feta on the bottom of the skewer so that it will be able to sit upright.

9   Place the Pesto directly on the platter and set the skewer on top of it.

10 To prepare the pickled red onion & pork bite, place the slice of pork directly on the platter and top with the pickled red onion.

APPENDIX

GARLIC CONFIT

Yield: 1½ Cups
Active Time: 10 to 15 Minutes
Total Time: 35 Minutes

Extra-virgin olive oil, as needed

Cloves from 5 heads of garlic

Salt, to taste

Pinch of red pepper flakes

Zest of ½ lemon

12 sprigs of fresh thyme

1 Warm a heavy-bottomed pot over medium-high heat and add enough olive oil to coat the bottom. Add the garlic.

2 Cook the garlic on medium heat for about 10 minutes, stirring occasionally and checking the heat to ensure the garlic is cooking evenly, until the garlic is a beautiful golden brown on all sides.

3 Add salt and the red pepper flakes. Stir to distribute.

4 Add olive oil until it fully covers the garlic. Add the lemon zest and thyme and turn the heat down to the lowest setting.

5 Continue to cook the garlic on very low heat for 20 to 30 minutes, or until the garlic is tender enough that you can easily crush it with a fork.

6 Store the garlic, covered in the oil, in the refrigerator until ready to serve. The garlic confit will keep in the refrigerator for up to 2 months.

2 tablespoons paprika

1 tablespoon granulated garlic

1 tablespoon granulated onion

1 tablespoon chili powder

1 tablespoon coriander

1 tablespoon dried thyme

1 teaspoon dry mustard

3 tablespoons brown sugar

1 teaspoon kosher salt

1 teaspoon cayenne pepper

1 teaspoon black pepper

BBQ RUB

1   Place all of the ingredients in a bowl and stir to combine, breaking up any large clumps of brown sugar. Use immediately or store in a dry, air-tight container.

Yield: ¾ Cup
Active Time: 15 Minutes
Total Time: 45 Minutes

½ cup sugar

½ cup water

SIMPLE SYRUP

1   Place the sugar and water in a small saucepan and bring to a boil, stirring to dissolve the sugar.

2   Reduce the heat so that the syrup simmers and cook for 1 minute.

3   Remove the pan from heat and let the syrup cool completely before using or storing in the refrigerator.

Yield: 8 Cups

Active Time: 20 Minutes

Total Time: 1 Hour and 20 Minutes

8 cups water

½ cup kosher salt

¼ cup sugar

BASIC BRINE

1   Place the water, salt, and sugar in a small saucepan and bring it to a gentle simmer, stirring to dissolve the sugar and salt.

2   Remove the pan from heat and let the brine cool completely before adding proteins or vegetables. If you want to add additional flavors to the brine, add those ingredients to the brine as it cools.

PICKLING SPICE

Yield: ½ Cup
Active Time: 10 Minutes
Total Time: 10 Minutes

1 tablespoon black peppercorns

1 tablespoon mustard seeds

1 tablespoon coriander seeds

1 tablespoon red pepper flakes

1 tablespoon dill seeds

1 tablespoon allspice berries

1 small cinnamon stick

10 bay leaves

1 tablespoon whole cloves

1 teaspoon ground ginger

1   Place the peppercorns, mustard seeds, and coriander seeds in a small dry skillet and toast over low heat until they are fragrant, 3 to 4 minutes, shaking the pan occasionally.

2   Transfer the toasted aromatics to a container, add the remaining ingredients, and stir to combine. Let the spice mixture cool completely before using or storing in an airtight container.

Yield: 1 Cup
Active Time: 5 Minutes
Total Time: 5 Minutes

4 oz. kosher salt

2 oz. sugar

2 teaspoons pink curing salt #1

STANDARD CURE

1   Place all of the ingredients in a bowl and stir until thoroughly combined. Use immediately or store in an airtight, nonreactive container.

PÂTÉ SPICE

Yield: 2½ Tablespoons
Active Time: 5 Minutes
Total Time: 5 Minutes

2 teaspoons cinnamon

1 teaspoon white pepper

1 teaspoon ground cloves

1 teaspoon freshly grated nutmeg

1 teaspoon ground ginger

1 teaspoon coriander

½ teaspoon dry mustard

1　Place all of the ingredients in a bowl and stir until thoroughly combined. Use immediately or store in an airtight container.

METRIC CONVERSIONS

WEIGHTS

1 oz. = 28 grams
2 oz. = 57 grams
4 oz. (¼ lb.) = 113 grams
8 oz. (½ lb.) = 227 grams
16 oz. (1 lb.) = 454 grams

VOLUME MEASURES

⅛ teaspoon = 0.6 ml
¼ teaspoon = 1.23 ml
½ teaspoon = 2.5 ml
1 teaspoon = 5 ml
1 tablespoon (3 teaspoons) = ½ fluid oz. = 15 ml
2 tablespoons = 1 fluid oz. = 29.5 ml
¼ cup (4 tablespoons) = 2 fluid oz. = 59 ml
⅓ cup (5⅓ tablespoons) = 2.7 fluid oz. = 80 ml
½ cup (8 tablespoons) = 4 fluid oz. = 120 ml
⅔ cup (10⅔ tablespoons) = 5.4 fluid oz. = 160 ml
¾ cup (12 tablespoons) = 6 fluid oz. = 180 ml
1 cup (16 tablespoons) = 8 fluid oz. = 240 ml

TEMPERATURE EQUIVALENTS

°F	°C	Gas Mark
225	110	¼
250	130	½
275	140	1
300	150	2
325	170	3
350	180	4
375	190	5
400	200	6
425	220	7
450	230	8
475	240	9
500	250	10

LENGTH MEASURES

¹⁄₁₆ inch = 1.6 mm
⅛ inch = 3 mm
¼ inch = 6.35 mm
½ inch = 1.25 cm
¾ inch = 2 cm
1 inch = 2.5 cm

INDEX

accompaniments, choosing, 7–8
agave nectar
    Hibiscus Sour, 130
Aioli
    Muffaletta Board, 174
    recipe, 177
almonds
    Bar Nuts, 129
almonds, chocolate-covered
    Date Night Board, 18
    Easter Board, 43
    On the Go Boards, 89
    Halloween Board, 144
    Picnic Board, 39
Angostura Bitters
    Hibiscus Sour, 130
apple chips
    Halloween Board, 144
    It's Gourd Season Board, 185
apples
    Baked Brie, 173
apricots, dried
    Fruit & Nut Board, 59
    Halloween Board, 144
    It's Gourd Season Board, 185
    Return of Spring Board, 15
    Stuffed Apricots, 60
    Valentine's Day Bouquet Board, 206
artichokes, marinated
    La Dolce Vita Board, 122
arugula
    Smoked Salmon Board, 52
asparagus
    Picked Asparagus, 17
    Return of Spring Board, 15
assembling charcuterie boards, 10
avocado
    Tuna Tartare, 97

Back to School Board, 125
Backyard BBQ Board, 79
bacon
    Bacon & Sage Caramel Corn, 235
    Bacon Jam, 31
    Burger Night Board, 29
    Choose Your Own Adventure Board, 75
    Movie Night Board, 232
Baked Brie
    recipe, 173
    Thanksgiving Board, 169
bananas
    Fourth of July Board, 81
Bar Nuts
    Cocktail Hour Board, 126
    recipe, 129
Basic Brine
    Confit Chicken Wings, 222
    recipe, 244
basil
    Pesto, 155
    Picked Asparagus, 17
    Tapenade, 176
    Tomato & Herb Focaccia, 161
    Vegetable Terrine, 164–165

BBQ Rub
    Pork Ribs, 84
    Pulled Pork, 80
BBQ Sauce
    Backyard BBQ Board, 79
    Pork Ribs, 84
    recipe, 242
Beach House Board, 111
beef
    Burger Night Board, 29
    Corned Beef, 229
    Smoked Beef, 68
    St. Patrick's Day Board, 227
    Summertime Is Here Board, 67
beer
    Country Mustard, 121
beets
    Beach House Board, 111
    Beet-Cured Salmon, 112
    Easter Board, 43
    Pickled Eggs, 45
    Roasted Baby Beets, 44
Birthday Board, 108
Blistered Shishito Peppers
    Cinco de Mayo Board, 46
    recipe, 51
blue cheese
    Blue Cheese Ranch, 226
    Labeled Charcuterie Board, 236
    Picnic Board, 39
    Super Bowl Board, 221
Blue Nights Board, 35
blueberries
    Fourth of July Board, 81
board materials, 9–10
Boursin cheese
    Mother's Day Board, 25
brandy
    Chicken Liver Pâté, 198
    Country Pork Pâté, 182–183
Bread & Butter Pickles
    Burger Night Board, 29
    recipe, 71
    Summertime Is Here Board, 67
brie cheese
    Baked Brie, 173
    Christmas Brie, 218
    Christmas Time Is Here Board, 217
    Date Night Board, 18
    Fruit & Nut Board, 59
    Labeled Charcuterie Board, 236
    Picnic Board, 39
    Return of Spring Board, 15
    Thanksgiving Board, 169
brioche buns
    Backyard BBQ Board, 79
Brûléed Fig & Goat Cheese Bites
    Harvest Board, 151
    recipe, 152
Burger Night Board, 29
burrata
    Dreams of Italy Board, 154
    It's Peach Season Board, 102
    La Dolce Vita Board, 122
    Return of Spring Board, 15
    see also mozzarella cheese

buttermilk
    Blue Cheese Ranch, 226
    Cornbread, 140
    Kimmelweck Rolls, 69

cabbage
    Fourth of July Board, 81
    Pickled Cabbage, 85
    St. Patrick's Day Board, 227
    Summertime Is Here Board, 67
Cabra cheese
    Spanish Tapas Board, 190
Candied Pecans
    Fruit & Nut Board, 59
    recipe, 63
Candied Pumpkin Seeds
    It's Gourd Season Board, 185
    recipe, 189
cantaloupe
    Blue Nights Board, 35
    Melon Shooter, 36
capers
    Smoked Salmon Board, 52
    Smoked Salmon Rillette, 115
    Tapenade, 176
capicola
    description of, 7
    Muffaletta Board, 174
    Return of Spring Board, 15
carrots
    Farmers Market Board, 162
    Super Bowl Board, 221
cashews
    Bar Nuts, 129
    It's the Holiday Season Wreath, 209
celery
    Farmers Market Board, 162
    Super Bowl Board, 221
Champagne
    It's a Celebration Board, 40
charcuterie
    Birthday Board, 108
    Entertaining a Large Group Board, 143
    Movie Night Board, 232
cheddar cheese
    Back to School Board, 125
    Christmas Time Is Here Board, 217
    Halloween Board, 144
    Labeled Charcuterie Board, 236
    Passed Hors d'Oeuvres Platter, 238–239
    Pimento Cheese, 136
    Potato Croquettes, 231
    St. Patrick's Day Board, 227
    Thanksgiving Board, 169
cheese
    Birthday Board, 108
    Cocktail Hour Board, 126
    Craft Night Board, 214
    description of, 7
    Entertaining a Large Group Board, 143
    On the Go Boards, 89
    It's a Celebration Board, 40
    Let's Celebrate Coupes, 205
    Movie Night Board, 232
    Stick to Tradition Board, 118
    Valentine's Day Bouquet Board, 206
    see also individual cheese types

cherries, dried
    Country Pork Pâté, 182–183
    Mother's Day Board, 25
chicharrón
    Cinco de Mayo Board, 46
chicken
    Confit Chicken Wings, 222
    Super Bowl Board, 221
Chicken Liver Pâté
    Elevated in a Pinch Board, 197
    recipe, 198
    Time to Shine Board, 178
chipotle peppers in adobo
    Chorizo, 48
Chive Crème Fraîche
    recipe, 56
    Smoked Salmon Board, 52
chives, fresh
    Blue Cheese Ranch, 226
    Chive Crème Fraîche, 56
    Pimento Cheese, 136
    Potato Croquettes, 231
    Smoked Salmon Rillette, 115
chocolate, dark
    Chocolate Cake, 145
    Chocolate Cake Truffles, 148
    see also almonds, chocolate-covered
Chocolate Cake Truffles
    Halloween Board, 144
    recipe, 148
Choose Your Own Adventure Board, 72
chorizo
    Cinco de Mayo Board, 46
    description of, 7
    recipe, 48
    Spanish Tapas Board, 190
Christmas Brie
    Christmas Time Is Here Board, 217
    recipe, 218
Christmas Time Is Here Board, 217
ciliegine
    La Dolce Vita Board, 122
Cinco de Mayo Board, 46
clementines
    Fruit & Nut Board, 59
Cocktail Hour Board, 126
cocoa powder
    Chocolate Cake, 145
coleslaw
    Backyard BBQ Board, 79
Confit Chicken Wings
    recipe, 222
    Super Bowl Board, 221
Cornbread
    recipe, 140
    Southern Tailgate Board, 134
Corned Beef
    red, 229
    St. Patrick's Day Board, 227
cornichons
    Cocktail Hour Board, 126
    French Countryside Board, 181
    Movie Night Board, 232
    Passed Hors d'Oeuvres Platter, 238–239
    Picnic Board, 39
    Time to Shine Board, 178

Country Mustard
    Labeled Charcuterie Board, 236
    recipe, 121
    Stick to Tradition Board, 118
    Summertime Is Here Board, 67
Country Pork Pâté
    French Countryside Board, 181
    It's Gourd Season Board, 185
    Labeled Charcuterie Board, 236
    recipe, 182–183
    Time to Shine Board, 178
Craft Night Board, 214
cranberries
    Cranberry Sauce, 170
cranberries, dried
    Baked Brie, 173
    Cranberry Goat Cheese, 213
    Date Night Board, 18
    Halloween Board, 144
    It's Gourd Season Board, 185
    It's the Holiday Season Wreath, 209
Cranberry Goat Cheese
    It's Gourd Season Board, 185
    It's the Holiday Season Wreath, 209
    recipe, 213
Cranberry Sauce
    recipe, 170
    Thanksgiving Board, 169
cream cheese
    Pimento Cheese, 136
    Smoked Salmon Rillette, 115
crème fraîche
    Chive Crème Fraîche, 56
    Smoked Salmon Board, 52
Cucumber & Mint Gin Rickeys
    Cocktail Hour Board, 126
    recipe, 133
Cucumber Mignonette Sauce
    Date Night Board, 18
    recipe, 21
cucumbers
    Bread & Butter Pickles, 71
    Cucumber & Mint Gin Rickeys, 133
    Cucumber Mignonette Sauce, 21
    Smoked Salmon Board, 52

Date Night Board, 18
dates
    Spanish Tapas Board, 190
    Stuffed Dates, 193
dill
    Blue Cheese Ranch, 226
    Bread & Butter Pickles, 71
    Need a Vacation Board, 199
    Smoked Salmon, 55
Dreams of Italy Board, 154

Easter Board, 43
Eat & Mingle Charcuterie Cups, 32
eggs/egg whites
    Aioli, 177
    Candied Pecans, 63
    Candied Pumpkin Seeds, 189
    Country Pork Pâté, 182–183
    Easter Board, 43
    Hibiscus Sour, 130
    Pickled Eggs, 45

    Pork Meatballs, 158
    Potato Croquettes, 231
Elevated in a Pinch Board, 197
Entertaining a Large Group Board, 143

Farmers Market Board, 162
feta cheese
    Eat & Mingle Charcuterie Cups, 32
    Passed Hors d'Oeuvres Platter, 238–239
    Summer Breeze Board, 90
figs
    Brûléed Fig & Goat Cheese Bites, 152
    Fruit & Nut Board, 59
    Harvest Board, 151
    Spanish Tapas Board, 190
fish and seafood
    Beach House Board, 111
    Beet-Cured Salmon, 112
    Labeled Charcuterie Board, 237
    Need a Vacation Board, 199
    Pickled Shrimp, 202
    Picnic Board, 39
    Smoked Salmon, 55
    Smoked Salmon Board, 52
    Smoked Salmon Rillette, 115
    Tuna Tartare, 97
Forbidden Black Rice Sprinkles
    National Ice Cream Day Board, 94
    recipe, 101
Fourth of July Board, 81
French Countryside Board, 181
fruit, dehydrated
    Entertaining a Large Group Board, 143
fruit, dried
    Back to School Board, 125
    Birthday Board, 108
    Craft Night Board, 214
    Let's Celebrate Coupes, 205
    Stick to Tradition Board, 118
    Valentine's Day Bouquet Board, 206
    see also individual fruits
fruit, fresh
    Birthday Board, 108
    Craft Night Board, 214
    Entertaining a Large Group Board, 143
    On the Go Boards, 89
    It's a Celebration Board, 40
    Watermelon Fruit Salad, 86
    see also individual fruits
Fruit & Nut Board, 59
fruit preserves
    Christmas Brie, 218
    Easter Board, 43
    Entertaining a Large Group Board, 143
    Picnic Board, 39
    Stick to Tradition Board, 118

garlic
    Blue Cheese Ranch, 226
    Bread & Butter Pickles, 71
    Corned Beef, 229
    Country Pork Pâté, 182–183
    Garlic Confit, 241
    Herb Mayo, 76
    Pork Meatballs, 158
    Smoked Beef, 68

Garlic Confit
    Aioli, 177
    La Dolce Vita Board, 122
    Pesto, 155
    Pimento Cheese, 136
    recipe, 241
Genoa salami
    La Dolce Vita Board, 122
    Muffaletta Board, 174
    Passed Hors d'Oeuvres Platter, 238–239
    Salami Roses, 26
giardiniera
    Tapenade, 176
Gin Rickeys, Cucumber & Mint, 133
ginger, fresh
    Preserved Peaches, 107
    Rhubarb Chutney, 16
    Tuna Tartare, 97
ginger liqueur
    Raspberry & Rose Sgroppino, 22
goat cheese
    Brûléed Fig & Goat Cheese Bites, 152
    Christmas Time Is Here Board, 217
    Cranberry Goat Cheese, 213
    Harvest Board, 151
    It's Gourd Season Board, 185
    It's the Holiday Season Wreath, 209
    Labeled Charcuterie Board, 236
    Passed Hors d'Oeuvres Platter, 238–239
    Picnic Board, 39
    Rosemary Goat Cheese, 210
gochujang
    Tuna Tartare, 97
gouda cheese
    Burger Night Board, 29
    Easter Board, 43
gravlax
    Need a Vacation Board, 199
green beans
    Farmers Market Board, 162
Grilled Peaches
    It's Peach Season Board, 102
    recipe, 104

Halloween Board, 144
ham
    Easter Board, 43
    Harvest Board, 151
    It's Peach Season Board, 102
    Passed Hors d'Oeuvres Platter, 238–239
    Return of Spring Board, 15
Harvest Board, 151
Herb Mayo
    Choose Your Own Adventure Board, 72
    recipe, 76
herbs, fresh
    Easter Board, 43
    Farmers Market Board, 162
    Herb Mayo, 76
    It's Gourd Season Board, 185
    It's the Holiday Season Wreath, 209
    Let's Celebrate Coupes, 205
    Return of Spring Board, 15
    see also individual herbs
Hibiscus Sour
    Cocktail Hour Board, 126
    recipe, 130

Homemade Hot Sauce
    recipe, 223
    Super Bowl Board, 221
honey
    Baked Brie, 173
    It's a Celebration Board, 40
    Labeled Charcuterie Board, 236
    Stick to Tradition Board, 118
hummus
    It's Gourd Season Board, 185
    Roasted Gourd Hummus, 186

ingredients
    choosing variety of, 7–8
    pairing, 8–9
    see also individual ingredients
It's a Celebration Board, 40
It's Peach Season Board, 102
It's Gourd Season Board, 185

kale
    It's the Holiday Season Wreath, 209
Kimmelweck Rolls
    recipe, 69
    Summertime Is Here Board, 67

La Dolce Vita Board, 122
Labeled Charcuterie Board, 236
lavender
    It's Peach Season Board, 102
    Lavender & Peach Jam, 106
    Valentine's Day Bouquet Board, 206
lemon juice/zest
    Aioli, 177
    Baked Brie, 173
    Brûléed Fig & Goat Cheese Bites, 152
    Chive Crème Fraîche, 56
    Cranberry Sauce, 170
    Cucumber Mignonette Sauce, 21
    Garlic Confit, 241
    Lavender & Peach Jam, 106
    OTL Burger Sauce, 30
    Pesto, 155
    Picked Asparagus, 17
    Pickled Shrimp, 202
    Pickled Watermelon Rind, 93
    Raspberry & Rose Sgroppino, 22
    Rhubarb Chutney, 16
    Roasted Gourd Hummus, 186
    Smoked Salmon, 55
    Stuffed Dates, 193
    Tapenade, 176
lemon peel
    Beet-Cured Salmon, 112
lemongrass
    Tuna Tartare, 97
Let's Celebrate Coupes, 205
lettuce
    Choose Your Own Adventure Board, 72
lime juice/zest
    Cucumber & Mint Gin Rickey, 133
    Hibiscus Sour, 130
    Melon Shooter, 36
    Tajín Crema, 49
    Tuna Tartare, 97
limes
    Cinco de Mayo Board, 46

Manchego cheese
    Eat & Mingle Charcuterie Cups, 32
    Mother's Day Board, 25
    Spanish Tapas Board, 190
mango
    Tuna Tartare, 97
maple syrup
    Roasted Gourd Hummus, 186
    Spicy Maple Bacon, 75
marinara sauce
    Stromboli, 224
mascarpone cheese
    Stuffed Apricots, 60
    Stuffed Dates, 193
mayonnaise
    Blue Cheese Ranch, 226
    Choose Your Own Adventure Board, 72
    Herb Mayo, 76
    OTL Burger Sauce, 30
    Pimento Cheese, 136
meat jerky
    It's a Celebration Board, 40
meats, cured
    choosing variety of, 7
    Dreams of Italy Board, 154
    On the Go Boards, 89
    Let's Celebrate Coupes, 205
    Stick to Tradition Board, 118
Melon Shooter
    Blue Nights Board, 35
    recipe, 36
metric conversions, 248
Mexican crema
    Tajín Crema, 49
mint, fresh
    Blue Nights Board, 35
    Cucumber & Mint Gin Rickey, 133
    Melon Shooter, 36
    Pesto, 155
    Summer Breeze Board, 90
    Valentine's Day Bouquet Board, 206
mortadella
    Muffaletta Board, 174
    Summer Breeze Board, 90
    Thanksgiving Board, 169
Mother's Day Board, 25
Movie Night Board, 232
mozzarella cheese
    Dreams of Italy Board, 154
    La Dolce Vita Board, 122
    Passed Hors d'Oeuvres Platter, 238–239
    Picnic Board, 39
    Super Bowl Board, 221
    see also burrata
Muffaletta Board, 174
mustard
    Entertaining a Large Group Board, 143
    French Countryside Board, 181
    Halloween Board, 144
    Summertime Is Here Board, 67
    Time to Shine Board, 178

nasturtiums
    Beach House Board, 111
    St. Patrick's Day Board, 227
National Ice Cream Day Board, 94

Need a Vacation Board, 199
nuts
    Birthday Board, 108
    Craft Night Board, 214
    Entertaining a Large Group Board, 143
    see also individual nut types

olives
    Eat & Mingle Charcuterie Cups, 32
    On the Go Boards, 89
    La Dolce Vita Board, 122
    Passed Hors d'Oeuvres Platter, 238–239
    Spanish Tapas Board, 190
    Tapenade, 176
On the Go Boards, 89
onions
    Bacon Jam, 31
    Burger Night Board, 29
    Chicken Liver Pâté, 198
    Chorizo, 48
    Country Pork Pâté, 182–183
    Homemade Hot Sauce, 223
    Pickled Cabbage, 85
    Pickled Red Onions, 139
    Pork Meatballs, 158
    Smoked Salmon Board, 52
    Southern Tailgate Board, 134
orange juice/zest
    Cranberry Sauce, 170
oranges, candied
    Craft Night Board, 214
    It's the Holiday Season Wreath, 209
    Return of Spring Board, 15
    Valentine's Day Bouquet Board, 206
oregano blossoms
    Mother's Day Board, 25
OTL Burger Sauce
    Burger Night Board, 29
    recipe, 30
oysters
    Date Night Board, 18

Parmesan cheese
    Pesto, 155
    Stromboli, 224
parsley, fresh
    Pesto, 155
Passed Hors d'Oeuvres Platter, 238–239
Pâté Spice
    Country Pork Pâté, 182–183
    recipe, 247
peach preserves/jam
    Labeled Charcuterie Board, 236
    Passed Hors d'Oeuvres Platter, 238–239
peaches
    Grilled Peaches, 104
    It's Peach Season Board, 102
    Lavender & Peach Jam, 106
    Preserved Peaches, 107
peanuts
    Bar Nuts, 129
pecans
    Baked Brie, 173
    Bar Nuts, 129
    Brûléed Fig & Goat Cheese Bites, 152
    Candied Pecans, 63
    Fruit & Nut Board, 59

Harvest Board, 151
pepperoni
    Date Night Board, 18
    La Dolce Vita Board, 122
    Passed Hors d'Oeuvres Platter, 238–239
    Stromboli, 224
    Super Bowl Board, 221
peppers, bell
    Farmers Market Board, 162
    Vegetable Terrine, 164–165
peppers, chile
    Homemade Hot Sauce, 223
peppers, peppadew
    Homemade Hot Sauce, 223
    Pimento Cheese, 136
peppers, pickled
    La Dolce Vita Board, 122
peppers, shishito
    Blistered Shishito Peppers, 51
    Cinco de Mayo Board, 46
Pesto
    Dreams of Italy Board, 154
    Passed Hors d'Oeuvres Platter, 238–239
    recipe, 155
Picked Asparagus
    recipe, 17
    Return of Spring Board, 15
Pickled Cabbage
    Fourth of July Board, 81
    recipe, 85
    St. Patrick's Day Board, 227
    Summertime Is Here Board, 67
Pickled Eggs
    Easter Board, 43
    recipe, 45
Pickled Red Onions
    Passed Hors d'Oeuvres Platter, 238–239
    recipe, 139
    Southern Tailgate Board, 134
Pickled Shrimp
    Need a Vacation Board, 199
    recipe, 202
pickled vegetables
    Entertaining a Large Group Board, 143
    It's a Celebration Board, 40
    Movie Night Board, 232
    Stick to Tradition Board, 118
Pickled Watermelon Rind
    recipe, 93
    Summer Breeze Board, 90
Pickling Spice
    Corned Beef, 229
    recipe, 245
    Smoked Beef, 68
Picnic Board, 39
Pimento Cheese
    It's the Holiday Season Wreath, 209
    recipe, 136
    Southern Tailgate Board, 134
pineapple, dried
    Bar Nuts, 129
pistachios
    Bar Nuts, 129
    Country Pork Pâté, 182–183
    Stuffed Apricots, 60
    Summer Breeze Board, 90

popcorn
    Bacon & Sage Caramel Corn, 235
    Movie Night Board, 232
pork
    Backyard BBQ Board, 79
    Chorizo, 48
    Country Pork Pâté, 182–183
    Dreams of Italy Board, 154
    Fourth of July Board, 81
    Pork Meatballs, 158
    Pork Ribs, 84
    Pulled Pork, 80
    Tasso Pork Tenderloin, 141
pork belly
    Spicy Maple Bacon, 75
pork rinds
    Cinco de Mayo Board, 46
Potato Croquettes
    recipe, 231
    St. Patrick's Day Board, 227
potato salad
    Fourth of July Board, 81
    Summertime Is Here Board, 67
Preserved Peaches
    It's Peach Season Board, 102
    recipe, 107
prosciutto
    Blue Nights Board, 35
    Christmas Time Is Here Board, 217
    Date Night Board, 18
    description of, 7
    Halloween Board, 144
    Harvest Board, 151
    La Dolce Vita Board, 122
    Muffaletta Board, 174
    Passed Hors d'Oeuvres Platter, 238–239
    Return of Spring Board, 15
    Spanish Tapas Board, 190
    Super Bowl Board, 221
    Thanksgiving Board, 169
    Valentine's Day Bouquet Board, 206
Prosecco
    Raspberry & Rose Sgroppino, 22
provolone cheese
    It's the Holiday Season Wreath, 209
    Muffaletta Board, 174
    Stromboli, 224
Pulled Pork
    Backyard BBQ Board, 79
    recipe, 80
pumpkin
    Roasted Gourd Hummus, 186
pumpkin seeds
    Candied Pumpkin Seeds, 189
    It's Gourd Season Board, 185

queso fresco
    Cinco de Mayo Board, 46

radishes
    Easter Board, 43
    Farmers Market Board, 162
raisins
    Christmas Time Is Here Board, 217
    On the Go Boards, 89
    It's the Holiday Season Wreath, 209
    Rhubarb Chutney, 16

Raspberry & Rose Sgroppino
    Date Night Board, 18
    recipe, 22
regional specialties, 7
Return of Spring Board, 15
Rhubarb Chutney
    recipe, 16
    Return of Spring Board, 15
Rice Sprinkles, Forbidden Black, 101
Roasted Baby Beets
    Easter Board, 43
    recipe, 44
Roasted Gourd Hummus
    It's Gourd Season Board, 185
    recipe, 186
rosemary, fresh
    Christmas Time Is Here Board, 217
    It's the Holiday Season Wreath, 209
    Roasted Baby Beets, 44
    Rosemary Goat Cheese, 210
    Smoked Beef, 68

sage, fresh
    Bacon & Sage Caramel Corn, 235
    Baked Brie, 173
    Country Pork Pâté, 182–183
    Smoked Beef, 68
salami
    Christmas Time Is Here Board, 217
    Cocktail Hour Board, 126
    Craft Night Board, 214
    description of, 7
    Easter Board, 43
    Eat & Mingle Charcuterie Cups, 32
    Halloween Board, 144
    It's the Holiday Season Wreath, 209
    La Dolce Vita Board, 122
    Mother's Day Board, 25
    Muffaletta Board, 174
    Passed Hors d'Oeuvres Platter, 238–239
    Salami Roses, 26
    Super Bowl Board, 221
    Valentine's Day Bouquet Board, 206
salmon
    Beach House Board, 111
    Beet-Cured Salmon, 112
    Smoked Salmon, 55
    Smoked Salmon Rillette, 115
salmon, smoked
    Beach House Board, 111
    Labeled Charcuterie Board, 237
    Need a Vacation Board, 199
    Picnic Board, 39
    Smoked Salmon, 55
    Smoked Salmon Board, 52
    Smoked Salmon Rillette, 115
salumi
    Dreams of Italy Board, 154
saucisson
    It's Gourd Season Board, 185
    Time to Shine Board, 178
sausage, cured
    description of, 7
    Halloween Board, 144
    Labeled Charcuterie Board, 236
    Picnic Board, 39
    Valentine's Day Bouquet Board, 206

seafood. see fish and seafood
seaweed salad
    Need a Vacation Board, 199
shallots
    Cucumber Mignonette Sauce, 21
shrimp
    Need a Vacation Board, 199
    Pickled Shrimp, 202
shrimp chips
    Beach House Board, 111
    Need a Vacation Board, 199
Simple Syrup
    Cucumber & Mint Gin Rickey, 133
    recipe, 243
Smoked Beef
    recipe, 68
    Summertime Is Here Board, 67
Smoked Salmon
    Beach House Board, 111
    Labeled Charcuterie Board, 237
    recipe, 55
    Smoked Salmon Board, 52
    Smoked Salmon Rillette, 115
soppressata
    Muffaletta Board, 174
sorbet, raspberry
    Raspberry & Rose Sgroppino, 22
sour cream
    Blue Cheese Ranch, 226
    Chocolate Cake, 145
    Potato Croquettes, 231
    Southern Tailgate Board, 134
    Spanish Tapas Board, 190
Spicy Maple Bacon
    Choose Your Own Adventure Board, 72
    recipe, 75
squash
    Roasted Gourd Hummus, 186
squash, yellow
    Farmers Market Board, 162
    Vegetable Terrine, 164–165
St. Patrick's Day Board, 227
Standard Cure
    recipe, 246
    Spicy Maple Bacon, 75
    Tasso Pork Tenderloin, 141
Stick to Tradition Board, 118
strawberries
    Date Night Board, 18
    Easter Board, 43
    Fourth of July Board, 81
    Return of Spring Board, 15
    Valentine's Day Bouquet Board, 206
Stromboli
    recipe, 224
    Super Bowl Board, 221
Stuffed Apricots
    Fruit & Nut Board, 59
    recipe, 60
Stuffed Dates
    recipe, 193
    Spanish Tapas Board, 190
styling charcuterie boards, 9–10
Summer Breeze Board, 90
Summertime Is Here Board, 67, 209
Super Bowl Board, 221

Tajín Crema
    Cinco de Mayo Board, 46
    recipe, 49
Tapenade
    Muffaletta Board, 174
    recipe, 176
Tasso Pork Tenderloin
    Passed Hors d'Oeuvres Platter, 238–239
    recipe, 141
    Southern Tailgate Board, 134
tequila
    Hibiscus Sour, 130
Thanksgiving Board, 169
thyme, fresh
    Corned Beef, 229
    Country Mustard, 121
    Country Pork Pâté, 182–183
    Easter Board, 43
    Garlic Confit, 241
    Pesto, 155
    Roasted Baby Beets, 44
    Smoked Beef, 68
Time to Shine Board, 178
Tomato Water Gelee
    Farmers Market Board, 162
    recipe, 166
tomatoes
    Burger Night Board, 29
    Choose Your Own Adventure Board, 72
    Dreams of Italy Board, 154
    Farmers Market Board, 162
    Tomato & Herb Focaccia, 161
    Tomato Water Gelee, 166
    Vegetable Terrine, 164–165
trail mix
    Fruit & Nut Board, 59
    Picnic Board, 39
Tuna Tartare
    National Ice Cream Day Board, 94
    recipe, 97
turkey
    Back to School Board, 125
    It's the Holiday Season Wreath, 209

Valentine's Day Bouquet Board, 206
Vegetable Terrine
    Farmers Market Board, 162
    Labeled Charcuterie Board, 236
    recipe, 164–165
vodka
    Raspberry & Rose Sgroppino, 22

watermelon
    Blue Nights Board, 35
    Fourth of July Board, 81
    Summer Breeze Board, 90
    Watermelon Fruit Salad, 86
Wonton Cones
    National Ice Cream Day Board, 94
    recipe, 98

zucchini
    Vegetable Terrine, 164–165

ABOUT THE AUTHORS

Alejandra and Jamison are a wife-and-husband duo with a love for bringing restaurant-caliber recipes into the home kitchen. Having first met while working at a farm-to-table restaurant, they have a deep passion for the culinary industry that translates to their everyday lives.

Alejandra is a food photographer and stylist, and Jamie is a trained chef and recipe developer with 15+ years of experience at restaurants such as The Inn at Little Washington and Market Table Bistro. Their blog, Off the Line, is packed with recipes that are fresh, feature seasonal ingredients, and integrate classic cooking techniques. The blog is focused on being approachable for the home cook, like Alejandra, and remarkable for the chef inside all of us, like Jamie.

Based in Northern Virginia, they enjoy visiting the best wineries and breweries around, taking daily walks, and exploring locally sourced ingredients. They believe that each meal, no matter how simple or elaborate, deserves to be a special moment that inspires.

ABOUT CIDER MILL PRESS BOOK PUBLISHERS

Good ideas ripen with time. From seed to harvest, Cider Mill Press brings fine reading, information, and entertainment together between the covers of its creatively crafted books. Our Cider Mill bears fruit twice a year, publishing a new crop of titles each spring and fall.

"Where Good Books Are Ready for Press"
501 Nelson Place
Nashville, Tennessee 37214

cidermillpress.com